Manifesting a New Life:

Real Life Stories Inspired by the Law of Attraction

Compiled by Patricia LeBlanc

Table of Content

Disclaimer

Every word in this book is based on the co-authors personal experience. The results they have achieved in their lives and shared in their chapters are not scientifically proven. The publisher nor the author assume any responsibility for the authors sharing within these private experiences with the world. Although the co-authors and publisher have made every effort to ensure that the information in this book was correct at press time, the author and publisher do not assume and hereby disclaim any liability to any party for any loss, damage, or disruption caused by errors or omissions, whether such errors or omissions result from negligence, accident, or any other cause.

The information provided within these pages is solely your responsibility of how to incorporate it into your life. Nothing in this book is a quick fix promise. This book is solely a platform for the authors and myself to share our experiences and spread a light upon the world and give tips and advice to those who choose to take it and place it within their lives. Nothing in this book is intended to replace any medical, psychological or financial advice. Each person's results may vary.

MANIFESTING A NEW LIFE

Compiled by **PATRICIA LEBLANC**

Gratitude

This book would not have been possible without the support of several amazing people.

First I need to start by saying a HUGE THANK YOU to all of my amazing co-authors Angela Ong, Anika Low, Arlene Pe Benito, BettyLou Nelson, Carol-Chantal Séguin, Erica Stepteau, Grace Cloyd, Jennifer Low, Julie Bourbeau, Liz Smart, Mariana Calleja, Maryetta Jones, MJ Villard, Nicole Cyr, Paula Johnson, Rachel Vdolek, Tamie M Joyce, Theresia Valoczy, Valentina Gjorgjievska and Vilma Salazar.

THANK YOU for your faith in me and for showing up willing to help make the world a better place. I am so proud of every single one of you and I really appreciate YOU. Without you, this book would not have been possible. Thank You! Thank You! Thank You!

THANK YOU Anna Giannone, Farahana Surya Namaskar, Lisa Harris Gore and Twyla Clarke for contributing your short manifesting story. I truly appreciate each one of you. THANK YOU!

MANIFESTING A NEW LIFE

I would not be where I am without my parents. My parents have taught me to never ever give up in life. Merci Mom et Dad pour tous les sacrifices que vous avez fait pour nous. Love you xoxo

To my dear friend Jennifer Low, Thank you! Thank you! Thank you! I am so grateful that you are in my life and that you make my writing look good. You are such a blessing not only in my personal life, but in my business as well.

To my close friends and inner circle, you know who you are, thank you so much for encouraging me to become a better person and to never ever give up on my dream. You have kept me going when I wanted to quit and it was quite often at times. From the bottom of my heart a huge THANK YOU! So GRATEFUL and BLESSED to have you all in my life.

Thank you Universe and my Angels for helping me manifest my dreams and living a happy and abundant life.

Finally, a huge thank you to each one of you who have purchased a copy of our book. My hope is that you will realize just how powerful you are and to start living life on your own terms. Your support means the world to us. I hope that you will enjoy our book and that it will change your life.

Much Gratitude and Love, Patricia xo

Compiled by **PATRICIA LEBLANC**

Introduction

Wow! I cannot believe that I am writing the introduction for the last book in the International Best Seller Series *Manifesting a New Life*. What a journey this has been.

Some of the lessons that I learned from creating this book series are that you need to stay aligned with your true self and soul, and that you need to keep going and never give up when you are faced with a challenge.

I came very close to quitting and pulling the plug on this entire project before it was even born. Boy, am I ever glad I didn't, as this life changing book series would have never seen the daylight. That is how bad I was tested.

This book series has been a life changer. It has changed my life and opened doors that I only dreamed about, but never believed could happen to me. It has changed the lives of my co-authors, but even more importantly it helped change other people's lives.

I am so blessed that I get to do what I love every single day. It wasn't that long ago that on the outside it looked like I was happy and successful, yet on the inside I was miserable and considered quitting everything that I worked so hard at.

MANIFESTING A NEW LIFE

When I started applying the law of attraction principles in my life as well as surrounding myself with amazing and uplifting people, magic started happening.

My intention with this book is to give women their power back. I want you to realize how powerful you truly are and that you can create the life and business that you truly desire.

I want you to start dreaming big! I want you to believe in the power of magic. I want you to know that you are worthy of creating the life and business that you desire. I want you to realize just how powerful you are and to start living a happy, fulfilled and abundant life. It is your time. Take it and make it yours!

Enjoy reading each chapter, as each one of my amazing co-authors will inspire you with their own manifesting story. They walk their talk and most of them have overcome the impossible and made their dreams come true.

Don't hesitate to reach out to me or to any of my co-authors of *Manifesting a New Life* if our story and chapter resonated with you. You will find all of their contact information and links within these pages.

So please read this book and then contact me at info@patricialeblanc.ca to let me know how it has helped you to move forward in your life and business, because I would love to know your success stories.

Here's to manifesting the life that you truly desire, because you are worthy of it!

Happy Manifesting!

MANIFESTING A NEW LIFE

Patricia LeBlanc

Patricia LeBlanc is a Dream Maker. She empowers Spiritual Female Entrepreneurs to get out of their own way so that they can create the life and business that they desire. Patricia helps her clients get clear on what they want, release their money blocks and charge what they are truly worth.

Patricia is an Award winning Author, Compiler and Publisher, International Speaker and Trainer, Manifesting and Business Strategist as well as a Master Energy Healer and Teacher.

Let Patricia help you like she has helped thousands before you. Apply for your free consultation by visiting www.YourAbundanceCoach.com/Consultation

You can contact Patricia by Email: info@patricialeblanc.ca Or info@manlpublishing.com

Chapter 1

How to Manifest Anything That you Truly Desire

By Patricia LeBlanc

Ever wonder why some people can manifest anything they want with ease and grace?
Why some people seem to be so lucky in life and get everything that they want?
Or why some people can manifest anything quickly?

You are not alone and these people are not any better than you. They just know how to manifest anything that they desire either on a conscious or subconscious level.

Once you learn some basic manifesting principles, you can learn how to use the law of attraction to manifest whatever your heart desires?

Let me share with you my step by step system that I have used to make all of my dreams come true, such as being CEO of my own business that supports me 100%, appearing on several online summits with so many amazing experts including my mentor Dr. Joe Vitale from *The Secret*, as well as co-authoring a book with him and so much more. I have also helped thousands of people use the law of attraction to create the life and business that they desire so that they can live a happy, fulfilled and abundant life.

You have the power to create the life and business that you truly desire. Are you ready? Awesome! Let's start!

You need to be Crystal Clear on what you want?

In order to manifest with ease and grace, you need to know what you truly want. Ask yourself the following questions:

- What does perfect health look like to for you?
- What does a perfect financial situation look like for you?
- What does your perfect business and/or professional life look like for you?
- What does your perfect lifestyle look like for you?
- What does your perfect spiritual and emotional life look like for you?
- What does your perfect family life look like for you?
- What does your perfect love life and relationships look like for you?

Once you know exactly what you want to create, you will be able to manifest what your heart truly desires.

MANIFESTING A NEW LIFE

I have a manifesting journal where I write everything that my heart desires. It is powerful to have it written down in one place. I like to splurge on my manifesting journal, but if you are on a budget you can buy one at a dollar store.

I am going to suggest that you set a few hours aside, and do the following exercise. You will need a journal, a quiet place where you will not be interrupted, some sage incense, a pen, and your favorite drink. You can also play some music. I put on either classical or dance music.

Once you have found your quiet place, sage the area. Sage actually helps to clear any negative energy that is around. You can also do energy clearing if you want. I normally do both, but either one is good. Once you have everything you need and you are settled in, meditate on each question and see what comes up. Journal your answers and do not stop and think about what is coming up and why. It is important that you let yourself go and let your intuition and soul take over, leaving your head out of it completely.

It is important that you go within to see what you truly want and not what others want for you. Most of us want something, because our parents, significant other, family member, friend or even society, tell us what it is that we want.

Don't stress if you do not figure it all out in one sitting. It may take you some time and the clarity will come to you in perfect divine timing. Make it a point of doing this exercise on a regular basis. The more often you do this the more clarity you will get.

Promise me that you will start putting yourself first and make time to figure out what you truly want. You are worthy of getting what you truly want.

Ask for what you want!

Once you know what you want, you need to ask for it. So many people skip this step. There are several ways that you can ask for what you want. You can ask the following ways:

- By asking the Universe (or Angels, God, Lord or whatever you call your higher power) out loud.
- By writing it down.
- By asking on Social Media
- By sharing it with your coach, mentor or mastermind group.
- By asking someone you know that can help you get to what you want.

Only share your dreams with people who will encourage and believe in you. Be careful who you share your dreams with.

MANIFESTING A NEW LIFE

Do not share your dreams with the naysayers, because they can drain your energy and help you block the manifestation from happening.

There is enough abundance for everyone so you can ask for anything.

Believe it will happen.

Have faith that it will happen in perfect divine timing. You will be tested by the Universe on how bad you want something and this is when having faith will be super important. When you believe that you can achieve it, you can. When you believe that it will never happen, it won't. It takes the exact same amount of energy to believe you can or believe that you cannot, so choose to believe that it will happen.

Take Inspired Action.

If you sit around and wait for whatever you want to appear in your lap, you will never get anything. It is so important to take inspired action. Ask your higher power for guidance and listen to what comes up. It can be an idea, a person or an opportunity that shows up for you. When it shows up, take action. If you don't know how, just jump in fully and watch the magic unfold right in front of you.

Have you ever had an idea that you did not act on only to find out later that someone else took action and made lots of money on the exact same idea? You want to know why? It's because the Universe will give the exact same idea to at least 10 people, because it knows that maybe, and I mean maybe, 1 of them will act on it.

So stop waiting until you have it all figured out. Jump in, and take inspired action.

Be open to receiving

This important step is left out by many people. In order to manifest whatever you desire, you need to be open to receive it when it arrives. This can be ideas, opportunities, and people who come into your life. Find yourself a quiet area and you can either mediate or sit in quietness and ask yourself, what is your capacity to receive (add whatever you want to manifest here). What answer are you getting? If you are not getting an answer at that time, be patient, as the answer will come to you in perfect divine timing.

The power of gratitude.

It is so important to always be in an energy of gratitude. A lot of people wait until they get what they want to say thank you. I always start my day by saying I love my life as well as

MANIFESTING A NEW LIFE

THANK YOU! THANK YOU! THANK YOU, Universe and Angels, for the gift of another day and I cannot wait to see what gifts you are sending me today. I also end the day by writing at least 10 to 15 things that I am grateful for. I start with 'I am happy and grateful that...' for each thing, opportunity and person. Make certain that you find something new each and every single day. Once a month I make time to write 100 things, people and opportunities that I am grateful for. This will help to speed up your manifesting power as well as raise your energetic vibration. Make the time today to do this and watch magic start happening, as you will be focusing on what is going well in your life instead of what is going wrong.

Always remember you have the power to manifest the life and business that you desire. You are that powerful of a creator! I believe in you! The question is do you believe in yourself and in your ability to create the life and business that you truly desire?

Happy Manifesting!

MJ Villard

Through her journey MJ Villard discovered a passion for inspiring and empowering women. She helps female entrepreneurs get out of their head and into their heart to awaken to their true nature, so they can live a purpose driven life and be world-class leaders in their business. Through her intuitive coaching system she guides them to create the business they truly desire and deserve. As a certified Ho'oponopono Practitioner she assists them to reconnect with themselves. Helping them clear limiting beliefs, take total responsibility, claim their power and truly fall in love with themselves, leading to self-improvement that will, in turn, better the world. She believes every woman should know they matter.

Let's start a conversation,
Email: mjvillard@live.ca
Facebook: www.facebook.com/mjvillard

Chapter 2

Everything Happens in Divine Timing

By MJ Villard

Growing up, I had a lot of anger inside of me. Anytime I was mad, I would scribble on a piece of paper. Although I was very good at languages, I wasn't very expressive. I just kept everything inside and would not share how I felt with anyone. I was an Ace at the Poker face game. I was a Master at making it seem as if everything was always ok. In my mind, if I had shared how I truly felt, people would have labeled me as weak. Being weak equalled being vulnerable. And at the time, I didn't understand the power that can come from vulnerability.

I was taught to always be strong and to put everything and everyone before my own self. And somehow by doing so, my life would just be so great. Because I was trying so hard to be everything to everyone, I couldn't really get in touch with who I really was and I definitely lost myself in the process. Deep down inside it never made sense, but that is what I was taught and I didn't know any better.

Compiled by **PATRICIA LEBLANC**

Things started to change as I began high school. When the time came to choose some courses. I felt compelled to sign up for literacy writing. Everyone including myself found it strange, as I was more of the athletic type. Going through that class was very empowering. For the first time in my life I could express my feelings and was able to pour my heart on paper. Whether I felt darkness, sadness, happiness or joy, taking my pen and paper would just put me in that place, that zone, where inspiration would flow with ease. It was as if someone had taken a huge weight off my shoulders. It was so freeing, so liberating. It was my self-made therapy. It made me able to cope with hardship and I fell in love with writing.

About a decade later, I consciously chose to start on my personal development journey. I was sick and tired of being sick and tired of going through life on other people's terms. I was fed up of not knowing what I truly wanted. I had it up to here of not living up to my true potential. I always had the belief that I was born for greatness. But in the society we live in, most of us are not raised to be trailblazers. Don't get me wrong, I am grateful for my parents. I believe they did the best they could with what they knew. As children, we grow up with what our family teaches us, but as adults, we volunteer to keep what they taught us, whether good or bad.

About 2 years ago I was sitting in a seminar and we were talking about money. The instructor made us come to the

19

realization that we all say we want more money, but in reality it's not the money that we want. It has to do with the freedom that comes with it. We were given an exercise, which consisted in answering questions to help us go deeper, to help us uncover our true purpose. Like most people do, I started to write that I wanted more money to buy the house and car of my dreams, to travel with my family, and all the material and superficial stuff. As I kept writing, I felt this very powerful flow of energy going through me, and with my watery eyes, I wrote the following:
- I want to touch thousands of people's lives
- I want to leave a legacy that even after I pass people will remember my name
- I want to write books in order to make a difference

I discovered that my purpose was to inspire women to open their heart and awaken their true nature and their true potential. I realized that my purpose was way bigger than me. It was exciting but frightening at the same time. Once I came to that realization, it became impossible to ignore. I had to face my true self. I was receiving what I had asked for.

The thought of writing just sat there, in the back of my mind. I left it at that, not knowing where or how to start. I just disciplined myself on working on who I have to become to live to my true potential. I stopped comparing myself to others, because honestly doing so is a recipe for disaster. I stopped blaming others and decided to take full responsibility for my life. Some would probably argue that everything that happens to you is not always 100% your fault since you have no control over others or on your environment. Although this is somewhat true, you can always choose how to react to what happens to you. The choice is not always obvious or easy, but it is there.

On my journey to self-discovery I experienced some ups and downs. Life has these ways of testing us on how bad we want what we say we want. With unwavering belief I stuck to it. As a matter of fact, I am still sticking to it.

At first, I was caught up in the *how*. Just thinking about it was so paralyzing, because I had no clue where to go or how to start. After a few months, I decided to let go of that control and surrender. Instead of trying to figure it out, I changed my questioning, which in turn shifted my mindset.

I started to ask myself empowering questions like: Who do I need to become in order to fulfill my purpose? What qualities would I need to have?

I embraced being perfectly imperfect. I meditated, I started a gratitude journal, I read books, and I surrounded myself with people who would elevate me. As I was moving forward, my vision became clearer and clearer. And I did all that from a place of love instead of ego. Not only for what it would bring me, but for how I could impact people if I was really being who I was meant to be. I just felt I was on my path with every fiber of my being.

On Thanksgiving 2016, Patricia LeBlanc and I were attending an executive's meeting for World of Women (WOW). As we were chatting, I shared for the first time, my dream of being a published author. The opportunity of being a co-author in Book 3 of *Manifesting a New Life* came up and as you can see, I gladly accepted. No need to tell you how grateful I am as I write these lines. As mentioned before, it was Thanksgiving Day. I could have easily declined to go, because of the Holiday. I could've said it's Thanksgiving and I am spending it with my family. But if I had done so, I wouldn't have had the opportunity of sharing my story with you today.

Sometimes in life we just have a strong feeling to take a certain action. It is so important to be able to quiet ourselves so we can hear our internal GPS. It's always there to guide us, but too often we either do not hear it or disregard it, because we are too much in our head. Know that your internal GPS, also known as your intuition, is always right. I am sure you could have a story or two to tell me on that from your own personal experiences.

Looking back, I realize there is no coincidence. Every moment led to the next. Whether it was taking that class or attending that seminar or going to that meeting where I had a conversation with Patricia LeBlanc. If you follow your intuition even if it does not make sense at first, it is preparing you for what is to come.

The most important lesson for me was to surrender and put my ego aside; that's when the magic happened. When you want something, when you ask, it is always given. Be patient with yourself and the process. Manifesting is not always instantaneous. Sometimes you need to go through challenges so you can build character to achieve what it is that you want to achieve. Don't sweat the small stuff. Align yourself with the frequency of what it is that you want. Be grateful for what you already have so you can allow more to come to you. I am here to tell you that you can manifest whatever it is that you want.

Small or big, on a vibrational level it is all the same. You cannot have or be what you are not willing to become. We can all thrive on 'never stop dreaming'. Let your light shine, have patience and trust that everything happens in divine timing.

MANIFESTING A NEW LIFE

Arlene Pe Benito

Arlene engages with her clients to mentor and empower those who find themselves stuck in the same patterns over and over. Through a simple process and a holistic approach, the root of the pattern is revealed and then transformed through several areas of their life: relationships, health and wealth. Arlene is a results-based coach, guaranteeing your results in writing.

Arlene is a Master Reiki Practitioner, Certified Master Teacher in Magnified Healing, Certified Master Neuro Linguistic Practitioner, Certified Master NLP Coach, Certified Master Time Line Therapist, Certified Master Hypnotherapist and Certified Trainer of Hypnotherapy, designated in over 38 countries.

You can contact Arlene via:

Email: livingwithcolour.coach@gmail.com
Website: www.livingwithcolour.coach
Facebook: https://www.facebook.com/arlene.p.benito

Chapter 3

We. Are. Powerful.

By Arlene Pe Benito

I have been working with the law of attraction for some time. I've read books and articles, I have had energy work done to clear my abundance blocks, I have used law of attraction rituals in my daily life, and I was really doing well with it. I was manifesting things beyond my belief. Every morning I would start my day by creating it, imagining what it was that I wanted to bring in and attracting it with emotion. Some days, I would ask for gifts, and they would arrive swiftly and on purpose. I received money, material things, things that I needed and things that I didn't. The world was my playground and it was unbelievable how easily things would come to me. I thought I had the law of attraction figured out. Sigh... I was wrong.

Words don't speak. Life experience speaks

I was a workaholic in a corporate setting, working fully to my physical and emotional means. My schedule was unstructured and I would work over night and during the day. My days were very long. I had little time for myself other than to sleep.

I spent about an hour a day with my children. As a one-income family, I justified it with my successes at work and the money that I was earning to support my family and me. Then I fell ill. I can't say that it was sudden, in fact, I saw it coming for several months, and I ignored the signs. It wasn't until I found myself uncontrollably crying every day that I finally sought help. I had avoided my negative emotions for so long that it grew to something I had no control over. I was diagnosed with depression and advised against my wishes to take time off of work. I led myself into such a state that I was no longer able to get out of bed, let alone care for my children or support them financially.

We are constantly creating and manifesting

Be it positive or negative, we are always attracting experiences into our lives with our present thoughts. It's based on our vibration and since we are vibrational beings, like attracts like. Our inner world is reflected in our outer world, and the negative experiences that we attract are an indication that we are in contrast to our true desires. I came to see that this experience was brought into my awareness to show me that I was misaligned with something in my life. Whenever I feel a negative emotion or physical pain, I am being asked to pay attention; this is my guidance system.

MANIFESTING A NEW LIFE

Recognize the contrast between what you want and what you have now

Having little time for myself and spending even less time with my daughters was excruciating. I would speak to them in the evenings while at work, and my children would cry, because they hadn't seen me or spent time with me. They mirrored what I felt, and with a brave face, I would explain that this was Mommy's job. Mommy's job was to create a life for us, so that we could do all of these wonderful things together. My emotions, body and experiences told me differently. I was lying to myself. There was no 'together'. In fact it was the opposite, and they saw right through it. My dream was to spend time with them, creating beautiful and loving memories. I craved a balance to raise them rather than just get them dressed and off to school with lunch in hand. I wanted to help them with homework, and be with them when they went to bed. I had aspirations to start my own business and be a successful entrepreneur. At that time, I was a Reiki Practitioner and my business plan included empowering others and myself. Years had gone by without any action, and it was tearing me apart. My inner being was screaming to be fulfilled, yet being busy at work allowed me to numb the pain that I was feeling inside. Funny enough, becoming depressed was probably the best thing to ever happen to me and my children. The reason is this: it forced me to stop and feel. I was forced to focus on me. It was now mandatory for me to look at my inner guidance system and see that I was not aligned. I was in flow of material things, while my body, mind and soul were missing a piece.

You create your own truths

For a long time after being diagnosed, I repeated my sad story, my hand on my furrowed brow for dramatic effect. I lived in the story of my past, as though it was happening day in and day out. I picked it apart, moment-by-moment, trying to identify how I got there. Deep analysis of the cause and the problem propelled me backwards, and the more conversations I had about it, the more confused I became. So I did the most courageous thing that I could do:

I sat.
And I sat some more.

I quieted my mind so that I could listen to my emotions and my body. I cut through all of the explanations, all the opinions of my friends and family, the advice of my therapist, including all the self blame, and just kept the emotion.

"Arlene, what are you telling me? How do I heal from this disease?" I asked myself, and I patiently awaited the answer.

MANIFESTING A NEW LIFE

The silence alone created a shift. No longer ignoring and simply being, brought relief. I received an answer and it was so simple. Promises I made to myself and to my children were unfulfilled. As such, I was living in contrast and what I had in my life, no longer filled my cup. I was ready for more. With a changed focus to the present rather than the past, my day-to-day perspective was positively affected. I shifted from depressed to guilt and in the time that followed, from guilt to sadness, and again from sadness to anger. I had to decide what I wanted, and bring it in to my experience accordingly.

When you ask, it is fulfilled

I wanted to be healthy, for when I became healthy, I would automatically become a better mom. My daughters had seen me at my lowest, and I wanted them to see me at my greatest.
I wanted to be the first face that my daughters saw in the morning. I wanted it to be joyful, excited and happy. I wanted to empower them and to show them that they could be whomever they wanted to be, and I was the prime example of that. I followed this vision and every day, little by little, my health improved. I saw the happiness start to spark and not just from within myself, from my daughters too. I was inspired! I was following my guidance system, and it was proving to be right!

Your emotional guidance system tells you if you are closer or further from your preferences

I was ready to start my holistic healing and coaching business. With increasing trust in my emotional guidance system, I took the actions that propelled me towards joy. I left my career of 10 years, grateful to everyone and to the opportunities. I had changed and the contrast was too great a distance for me to stay. As I started to become aligned, windows of opportunity came forth. I put out my intention, which was to empower others using holistic healing and coaching techniques. I was to positively impact each and every person that I met. I was to change the world. Opportunities for growth and to fulfill my intentions came forward and it was up to me to take action towards them, using my guidance system along the way. One opportunity that I attracted was a book deal. In fact, I attracted two! I had always wanted to be an author, I didn't know how I was going to make that happen, and I attracted it to me! Learning opportunities, clients, mentors, and friends. I asked, it showed up!

When you are present, success is inevitable

It is in the present moment that you can follow your inner guidance system. It is here to provide you with contrast. It doesn't mean that negative emotion is bad, it is simply telling you to stop in that moment and look around. What you are seeing, feeling and thinking may be something that you want to move away from, and you have the power to do it. It's just that simple. Moving towards your joy-filled thoughts and actions attract more of the same. My guidance system led me to consciously manifest a new life filled with health, wealth and happiness. The most amazing thing out of all of this, is that I now attract those who want to become empowered, be the best version of themselves and manifest their new life.

Grace Cloyd

Grace Cloyd is an astrologer-numerologist, intuitive reader-advisor, astrology-numerology blogger, and author. Her practice, Life By Soul™, is based in San Jose, CA. She has developed her own blend of Western Astrology and Latin Numerology called *The Life By Soul™ System* which she uses effectively to her clients' benefit, development, and growth. You can learn more about her and her work at her main website http://www.lifebysoul.com and the Life By Soul™ social media pages at www.facebook.com/lifebysoul and http://twitter.com/lifebysoul.

Chapter 4

Take the Leap! - Expect the "Worst" and Do Your Best

By Grace Cloyd

Whenever I've focused too hard on a goal or an outcome I've wanted to manifest, I've noticed that I get too emotionally invested, caught up in my self-created hype and panic, and become so anxious and stressed out, I end up self-sabotaging or imploding on myself.

Through those experiences, I finally learned that when I do manifest my intentions and goals, it's in the times when I let go.

I don't mean set an intention or say a prayer then do nothing while waiting for it to show up in front of me. Oh no. I still get to take action to progress myself toward my goals, to position myself to fulfill upon my intentions. What I mean by 'let go' is that I release my attachment to the outcome, and I recognize and accept the fact that I'll still be who I am with or without the desired result being achieved.

My mantra in everything I do is, "Expect the worst and do your best." The reason this works for me is because it shifts my mind away from trying and toward *being*. I'm no longer trying to succeed – I'm just *being* the best expression of my true self that I can be in that moment. I am being my authentic self when I take intentional action, and that makes all the difference for me.

The best manifestations – for me – often come as a result of taking what I consider to be 'long-shot chances' on myself. I get an idea in my head that won't go away, and eventually I decide, "I might as well go for it." I figure the worst someone could tell me is "no" and the worst thing that could happen is I may fail, so I choose to jump off the proverbial cliff knowing once I take that leap, there's no going back. Only forward.
The funny thing is…when I take those leaps, that's when the magic happens.

A leap of courage

When I was 18, I auditioned for the color guard of a world-class performance group I had admired for years. Despite my seven years of prior guard experience, I didn't think I had the right experience, the right connections, the necessary degree of talent, the right look… This was one of the best performance groups in the world, and I was coming in, in my mind, from nowhere. After panic upon panic, at the urging of my brother and a lifelong friend, I finally sucked it up and went in to audition.

I went in expecting the worst but giving it my best without expectation of success or return. I just knew I had to give it my all, and whatever happened would happen.

Well, my audition turned into a call back, which turned into another call back, which turned into another. I was called back every weekend for three months until they told me I'd earned a spot. That's how I started marching for the Concord Blue Devils Drum and Bugle "A" Corps Color Guard. We were the champion color guard that year in 1992, and two years later in 1994, we were part of the organization's seventh full corps DCI World Championship title.

A leap of initiative

Flash-forward 10 years, I had moved back to my childhood home after living in Los Angeles for 6 years. I was dealing with a severe intestinal illness, and needed a place to stay while I was treating and recovering.

As my health improved, I needed to work. I had used all of my savings on health care, so I had nothing – I was starting life from scratch. To get myself back on track, I returned to a temp employment agency I had worked with before I moved away. Before I went in, I wrote my job criteria in my journal – it needed to be within walking distance of home, pay a certain amount, have decent hours, and be a relatively stress-free environment. The agency took my updated info and tested my skills. Within a week, I had a temp job, which (unbeknownst to the agency) met all of my criteria to a tee! It was the transition work I needed to get myself up and running again.

A leap of faith

About three years later, I moved to San Jose and the new work-from-home job I had wasn't enough to pay my bills. I had been doing numerology, astrology, and tarot as hobbies for over 20 years, always willing to do charts and readings for friends. It would often result in them saying "You should do this for a living", but I really couldn't wrap my brain around doing it as my profession.

Yet a few months later, figuring I had nothing to lose, I went for it. I was speaking with one my best friends (from the color guard days) who now happens to be an extraordinary graphic designer, and mentioned to him that I had decided to start an astrology-numerology practice. I think he was more excited than I was, and immediately offered to design my business logo. Then I mentioned to my roommate at the time that I needed to build a website, and she offered to assist me in getting a site up and running. Another friend offered to host my website on his private server, free of charge, and another friend knew a guy down the hall from her office who had a card printing special – I was able to get my first 500 business cards for $30.

The moment the website went up in June 2010 is the moment I consider Life By Soul was born, but not yet fully confident in my ability to be fully self-employed, I still took a couple of day jobs after I started Life By Soul. About 18 months later, I was laid off. It was such a relief – like a huge burden was taken off my shoulders... though I was still a bit concerned about how I'd support myself.

A leap of trust

About two weeks after the layoff, I walked out of a hair appointment and decided to visit a new metaphysical shop I'd been meaning to check out for a couple of months. I didn't have any expectations or intentions other than to check it out and see what they had to offer.

I entered, and the lady behind the counter asked me if I needed assistance. I said "No thanks. Just looking around." Then about 10 minutes later, she said, "You do something. What do you do?" I somehow knew she was speaking in metaphysical terms and I told her, "I'm an astrologer-numerologist and intuitive reader". She smiled and said, "Funny. We had an astrologer here – she was coming over the hill from Santa Cruz each week. She quit the other day, because she hated making the drive." After a short pause, she asked me, "Would you like to be the astrologer for the store?" She introduced herself as the owner, we talked for a little bit, exchanged business cards, and now, after four years, I continue to be available for readings at the store every Thursday. I am so blessed to be part of that community, and grateful that the owner took the chance on me... which she wouldn't have been able to do had I not trusted and honored my intuition to go into the store that day.

And I still have Life By Soul – my own practice – outside the store as well. It has grown through regular phone and in-person clients. Also, my first astrology-numerology book was released in 2016, and a few more books and an online course series are on the way.

My manifestations over the years have taught me two things:
1) I've learned that the Universe helps those who help themselves. I've learned that when I take leaps forward, honoring my inner truth and "expecting the worst and doing my best", I'm often pleased with the outcome.

2) I've also learned that the Universe synchronistically provides for me when I'm acting in alignment with my truth. Everything I truly need is given to me in the perfect way and at the perfect time when I am clear about my intentions and when my intentions are aligned with my authentic self-expression.

I still have to work for it. I still need to show that I have the desire to fulfill the ambition. I don't get to sit around and wait for things to come to me. I get to give things my best shot. I've learned through all of my experiences that it's really true – "if you never try, you'll never know".

Give yourself a chance! Take a chance on you! Take the leap! "Expect the worst and do your best"…and *you* may surprise *yourself* by allowing yourself to see how capable and amazing you are.

In fact, things may work out better than you ever could have imagined.

~ Light, Love, and Blessings to you,
Grace

Nicole Cyr

Nicole is an inspirational speaker and coach. She studied Non Violent Communication and is a certified Lifestyle Transformation graduate of the Hippocrates Health Institutes.

After living through many life traumas and witnessing her own healing through personal growth, work and team support, Nicole now assists others in healing themselves. She helps them to get past their survival stage and to attain the next step in order for them to thrive. She inspires people to co-create and manifest the life of their dreams with passion, joy, vitality and a deep fulfilling purpose.

Her daily motto is **Be Your Own Legend**!

Email: nicolecyrcoach@gmail.com

https://www.linkedin.com/in/nicolecyrcoach?trk=nav_respons ive_tab_profile

https://www.facebook.com/nicole.cyr.10

Chapter 5

The Unfolding of a New Life

By Nicole Cyr

I've had enough!

That's how I woke up the morning I was attending the first day of my 3ᴿᴰ Millionaire Mind Intensive weekend. I had been implementing it all: the positive thinking, the visualising, the vision boarding, the subliminal audios, the affirmations, releasing the past... I looked up to the ceiling of my room and said: "Universe! Listen to me! I want to know, once and for all, will I live a life of abundance one day? YES or NO? Be clear, please!"

It all started a year ago, when I saw an ad on Facebook announcing that Louise Hay was releasing 100 free conferences and 12 free movies during 3 weeks in May. What perfect timing! I had just finish years of recovery on so many issues.

After all that deliberate clean up, I was ready for some reprogramming and gearing myself towards a new positive life. I literally plugged myself in on a 21 day positive brainwash, like a "Reboot" on a computer that was installing new software. When I wasn't in the shower or at work or with my daughter, I was PLUGGED! For 21 days straight, I immersed myself in that positive vortex of energy.

3 weeks later, I saw an ad for a free seminar on how to become a millionaire.
Initial reflex: "YA RIGHT! Becoming a millionaire! ...and my name is Santa Claus?! Come on!" And then there was this new other voice that said: "Hey! You have been listening to 3 weeks of abundance material. Why not try it? There is no fee to attend. What do you have to lose?"
So I went. And that Millionaire Mind Intensive weekend changed my life forever!

The material covered in the three days was already intense and amazing to begin with, but wait, it gets better! That weekend, I met a woman who offered me an opportunity to join her MLM team and working it part time, I began making 500$ a month! Wow! The best part was that I was happy without a man, I was happy with the relationship I was having with myself, and I was happy in the skin I was in. I was finally experiencing what it felt like to live *happy* on a regular basis. I was so grateful. The brainwashing had worked after all!

MANIFESTING A NEW LIFE

But then, I was in for a surprise...

After that summer, my daughter who was now 15, wanted to go meet her maternal grand mother to reconnect after not having had any contact for 10 years. My role was just to be the driver and supervise in silence while they interacted.

The day after we visited my mom, I was struck with a sudden onset of depression, but there seemed to be no reasoning behind it. And then it hit me like a brick!

The memory of my mom's abuse came back. I felt like throwing up. The energy was sucking me from the bottom like a vacuum... NOOOO! I knew that trail only too well. Memories of a rich pedophile whom my parents were lending me out to when I was 4, came back to me. Every time, it was the same scenario: I was going there for an afternoon and I had 3 'clients' to service. And if I was not doing it correctly, the rich man would bring me to the basement and beat me. In the stomach. So it would leave no trace. I was suffering like hell.... again!

I felt discouraged. The fear of not regaining that happy state came over me. "I'm a warrior!" I told myself and fought my way through. That's when I realised that life had protected me. If I would have had those memories come to me before now, I don't think I would have dealt with them in quite the same way. I was now strong enough and enlightened enough, and I surrounded myself with spiritual life to clean up that chapter.

When I spoke to the Universe that morning, I was dead serious. I was a tired warrior who needed some rest. And off I went to attend the seminar.

After lunch, the trainer said to us: "I don't understand, when I was asking who was interested in that course there were about 150 hands up and I only had 2 registrations. How come?" And the group began: "it's too far, it's in US currency, I don't have the time, I have kids..."

Like a volcano irrupting in my belly, rage was coming up my throat. I put up my hand really high and I spoke up. I said with a trembling voice: "I'm a single mom and this is my 3rd time attending this event. I do all I can to have a better life. At the first one I was crying, because I was seeing the opportunities and I couldn't take them. I had no money, no credit. Nothing! You say that if I want to be a millionaire, I need to get out of my shit. You tell me to do something, to take action, any action and the Universe is just going to respond to me..."

Everyone was so fixated on what I was saying, you could have heard a pin drop.

MANIFESTING A NEW LIFE

I piped up: "And you know what? One day, maybe... NO! One day I WILL attend that course!" And I sat down, crumbling, crying, nursing my deep wounds regarding money...

And then... like Moses parting the sea, the Universe spoke to me!

A man stood up and said: "My name is Martin. I did all those courses and they changed my life. Ma'am, I don't know you, but I can feel all the determination, the courage and the engagement you have to change your life. I will buy you that course. I carried on crying. I was shaking from every cell of my body. I was so deeply touched.

Once the crowd had calmed down, the trainer followed this win with a prize draw for an iPad. He was about to take a ticket, but incidentally, one of them 'jumped out' of the jar and fell on the floor. Guided by the divine, that was the one he was compelled to call out. Still flooded in tears, I couldn't see the numbers on my ticket. As I wiped my face I kept repeating "74" in my head, which were the last two digits on my ticket. And low and behold, I had the winning ticket!!

The crowd was delirious. Some people were crying, some were stunned. We all knew that something magical had just happened. It was insane!

Later, I went up to Martin and I told him that not only was I grateful for the course he had so gracefully paid for me, but that with this single gesture, he had helped me pulverise my limiting beliefs around money once and for all. I felt the Universe was in my camp! This experience changed my life forever. I now believed I could live in abundance.

Instantly, I assisted in fascination to the unfolding of my life. Another seminar attendee came to me and asked me if I would like to be one of the featured speakers for an upcoming event. I said YES! I knew all I had to do was surf on the wave, stay in that vortex of energy, and follow the signs.

A day later, I bumped into someone I knew who invited me to dinner. Martin was there. It was fantastic to see him again. A few days after that, I attended an event where I won a course on how to trade the Stock Market. Following this, I received a random gift from a friend: a book called The Presence. A few days later, feeling a little bout of the blues, I asked the Universe if it loved me. Immediately, I receive a text from someone I hadn't seen in a long time. The only words displayed were "I love you." I was on a serious winning streak!

With such a big momentum in play, I continued to help the Universe move me forward even quicker: I started taking massive action in my own life. I deciphered what I had to offer the world and prepared business cards. I was in essence pre-paving my path. The Universe kept on delivering: a lady accepted to do my LinkedIn profile for free, and then I was asked to co-author in this book.

I am grateful to the Universe, for it cracked open the shell that was surrounding me. The seed that was germinating for years became a sprout, and just by following the sun, I am assisting with wonder, to the growth of a beautiful plant: my new life!

Whatever you are going through, please hang on. You have a unique seed inside of you that is waiting to find the right way to bloom. Stay strong, be faithful. Help is on its way.

Abundance!

...to be continued!

Compiled by **PATRICIA LEBLANC**

Short Manifesting Story #1

Once Upon a dream...

By Anna Giannone

In my early 20s it seemed I wasn't going anywhere in life. I didn't know how to overcome this relentless feeling of angst, or how to handle the hardships that I had been facing. The only thing I had to hang on to, was believing that one day my life would change. I knew it required courage and action to manifest this shift.

In 1976, I saw the movie about a boxer named Rocky. Somehow, I related to him when he was discouraged and felt worthless, as he had the willpower to overcome all the discouraging circumstances life kept throwing at him. The Rocky story was my self-help guidance. The courage he had to keep moving forward gave me goosebumps and he ultimately succeeded in the end. He inspired me to believe that it was truly possible to manifest one's dreams.

I convinced myself that one day I would somehow meet Rocky, played by Stallone. During my vacation in Beverly Hills, I discovered that he lived in the area, and I kept hoping I would meet him in a restaurant or on the streets, and we would chat on end about life! However, by the end of my trip, I never ran into my Rocky. I couldn't understand, I felt it so strongly in my gut that I would meet him. So I decided that I wasn't going to lose hope.

In July 1998, a Planet Hollywood restaurant in Montreal's downtown area was opening, and it was announced that Stallone was going to be there. Every day during lunch hour, I would take my daily walks and see the construction evolve, picturing myself finally meeting my Rocky. I would whisper back to my soul and say, "This is it. I will meet him."

I arrived early Saturday morning for the grand opening and finally, towards the end of the day, the actors that flew in for the opening were walking down the street. And then I heard it. The Rocky theme music. He walked down the street right up to me, and shook my hand! I was in awe as he winked and actually said hello. WOW, I thought, it finally happened. I knew it, I knew it!

Manifesting your dreams is possible. I finally understood that you have to believe it deep down. Sometimes it requires taking big steps or getting out of your comfort zone to make it happen. And especially, don't let anyone tell you that dreams are not possible. Believe in your dreams and they will manifest themselves in conjunction with the effort that you put into them.

Ever since that day, I strongly believe in the power of my dreams and that if I kept an open mind and applied myself to them, then I had a chance at seeing them come true. They are the answers to my heart's desires, and I know I am guided on the right path whenever they are calling.

MANIFESTING A NEW LIFE

Compiled by **PATRICIA LEBLANC**

Anika Low

Anika has been riding competitively for over 8 years and has acquired many precious life skills from her sport, which she gracefully incorporates into her everyday life. She is currently in her first year of high school and holds a brown belt advanced in Karate. Anika loves horses and is passionate about drawing Anime.

You can go view her art at:
www.daisusky.com

Chapter 6

Taking it in Strides

By Anika Low

I am thirteen years old and this is not the first time I have been published. You may be thinking that I am too young to be writing about manifesting and that I have not had many experiences to speak of. Yes, that may be true, but I have learned many life skills through the experiences my sport has offered me.

I have been horseback riding competitively for nine years and it has given me great skills that I use regularly in my everyday life.

Manifesting is one of those many skills.... It starts with a goal in mind. Then it needs to be followed up with the right mindset, the right actions, the right energy, hard work, and dedication.

One day, in the summer of my sixth competitive year, I was at a competition. It was a horse show like many other horse shows. My usual goal was to do well, with the intention of performing at my personal best and hopefully bringing home first place. I had a good mindset, and I already had all of the training I could have had for that day.

I prepared my horse in his clean show gear, warmed him up, did a practice round over the jumps and then went on to do my judged courses. My first round over the jumps was awesome. I was confident I had done a good job with my pony, Raisin. I believe I did even better on my second round. My third course was going great. Raisin and I were completely in sync with one another. We were working together, we were clearing the poles, we looked very good, and I was proud of myself that I was working so hard at keeping him straight to all the jumps. I was coming to my last jump and I soared over it, but while I was in mid-air I realized we had gone over the wrong one. Whatever points I had scored for that flawless last round were taken away from me and I was disqualified for that third class, because I was "off course". I was devastated.

I walked out of the ring with a tight jaw. I was so angry. I was holding back my tears, and I did not want to talk to anyone. I went past my coach by the in-gate. She wasn't nearly as upset as I was. In fact, she was quite proud of my riding and my overall decision-making. She instructed me to go cool off in the shade of the indoor arena. I think she understood that I needed a moment.

MANIFESTING A NEW LIFE

I went to walk my horse around in the arena to help him catch his breath and to relax myself. As I walked around, I noticed how patient and obedient my Raisin was, just like any other horse. I turned my attention to myself for a second and realized how awful my energy was. I noticed that my mindset got messed up after that course. All I was thinking about was obsessively reliving a moment that had already passed. I was still carrying that "upsetness" from my mess up with that last jump. I thought to myself that Raisin should not be punished for doing something I told him to do. I am the one who led him to that jump. I needed to take responsibility and be grateful that my pony was amazing at what he does and that he listens so well and keeps me safe that way. He had done what I told him to do in a perfect manner and should be praised for it. Animals that you are close to (and humans alike for that matter) can feel your energy and are affected by that energy.

I restored my good mood, my happy energy, and got my mindset back in place by the time I was leaving the coolness of the shady arena to return to the ring for my very last class of the day. I definitely had the determination to keep going and to finish off the day strong. That meant no matter what the outcome of the day was, I was glad, because I had learned a valuable lesson about myself that day. I learned that holding on to negative energy did not serve me. In fact, it hindered me to move forward freely and to do better next time.

With that, I walked into the ring with a happy and positive energy. I was proud of my pony. In this last class, it was an opportunity to show him off to the judge as being the best moving pony and the best living pony on the planet. I did just that!

Not only did I win that class, but even with the disqualification of that last jumping course, I had accumulated the most amount of points for the day in my division. This meant I had ridden my best that day and the outcome of all this was that I was bringing back the champion ribbon for the 2' jumping division. I had made this happen! By changing my energy and my mindset, I had manifested it and was being greatly rewarded for it.

I have to say, that being called back in the ring to collect my champion ribbon really drove the entire lesson home. Energy can have a domino effect whether it be positive or negative. People's energy affects other's energy, and your feelings and mindset affect your own energy. It is not fair for someone else to be punished by your energy and you should not punish yourself either. Pick yourself back up and carry on by learning from your mistakes rather than getting stuck on them.

Now, whenever I mess up during a course, I do not hold onto that mistake, because I know there is nothing I can do about it. The moment has passed. I have to focus on what is coming next. This works with anything you do in life too. When people hold on to grudges or mistakes then they are living in the past and cannot deal with the other problems that are coming next. Time does not stop for anyone.

Riding has taught me many life lessons and still does... with every ride. From this experience, however, I have learned to stay calm in tough situations and to truly 'let go' in order to move on.

I deliberately create my life and manifesting comes easily to me.

Vilma Salazar

Vilma has a lovely, bubbly personality and a warm, welcoming smile. She is passionate about making people look and feel their best. After an unexpected lay off at age 60, she embarked on an entirely new career, and a quest for time freedom and financial freedom.

For Vilma, it is not only about creating a sustainable income for herself and her family, but it is also about focusing her energy on mentoring others with a purity of intention, which fills her heart with joy. She strongly believes that anyone can create a new life and realize a new dream no matter their age.

Email: vilms2010@hotmail.com
Website: www.vsalazar.myrandf.com/ca
Website: www.vsalazar.myrandf.biz/ca

Chapter 7

It's Never too Late to Start Over

By Vilma Salazar

Growing up in Peru, I had an amazing childhood. I was raised by my grandmother until the age of 13. She was a wonderful soul who taught me to be generous, loving and compassionate. During my teenage years, I lived in Puerto Rico with my aunt, and returned to Peru at age 18. My first job was as an Executive Secretary to the Comptroller at the Lima Sheraton Hotel. I was 19. Life was perfect!

I got married at 25 and we had two beautiful sons. After 13 years of coping with an abusive husband, and fearing for my life, I got the courage to leave and took my sons with me. It was 1991, and there was another big threat: terrorism. Peru was unsafe.

I'll never forget the day my friend Linda called me. Our kids attended the same school. She told me: "Come to the school!" I knew that something bad must have happened. I ran to the school three blocks away. When I arrived, I saw it was surrounded by army tanks. My heart was beating fast. There had been a bomb threat and the kids were still inside! I felt so frightened and helpless! I could not continue living in fear. I prayed for an answer while asking myself: "What am I going to do?" I needed to get my kids to safety. But... where was I to go?

At the time, I was working for a reputable adoption lawyer as a translator and coordinator for Canadian and American couples looking to fulfill their dream of becoming parents. I assisted them through the whole adoption process, which was sometimes long and painful. Working closely with them allowed us to develop strong relationships.

I decided to ask them for help and advice on how to immigrate to Canada. I was fortunate that they were all willing to help me. I ended up with beautiful letters of recommendation written on my behalf, which I included with my Canadian resident visa application. I did not know if they would accept me, but I knew if it was meant to happen, it would.

The day of my interview, I was feeling great. I was leaving it all in the hands of God, and my faith told me that He would provide the best solution for me and for my children. Some of the applicants had diplomas and degrees. I didn't. I could see a couple of them being denied their visas and that made me anxious, thinking I was going to be rejected too!

MANIFESTING A NEW LIFE

My name was called and a French-Canadian officer interviewed me. He told me it might be better if I went to Canada by myself, and once I was established, I could bring my kids. I thought he must be crazy! How could I possibly leave my kids in Peru while I was safely in Canada? The whole purpose of immigrating was to provide a safe environment for my children. There was no way I was leaving them behind. I looked at him and said: "If I can't bring my children with me, then I'm not interested in the visa." He looked at me and smiled. Without saying a word, he kept writing on my application. I thought I blew it. I was certain that my visa application was going to be denied. He kept writing, and I was still looking at him. I interrupted that silence and courageously asked: "So... am I granted the visa?" He looked at me and said, "Have a seat ma'am. You will be called for your medical."

I was going to Canada with my kids!

We arrived in Canada in April of 1996. Terrorism had decreased in Peru and the country was recuperating, but as a result of a change of Government, I had lost my job. It was the perfect time to make a move and start fresh. I sold our apartment, car, and anything else I had. I was gearing up to making a fresh start in a new country.

One year passed in Canada and still, no job. Again, uncertainty touched my life. I was doing some translation work here and there, but not enough to make a living. I came close to having to move back to Peru, because I was running out of money. It was stressful having little income with two children who depended solely on me. I needed to make it happen for my sons. I prayed for a job.

My dad and brother came to visit me during our first Christmas in Canada. One morning, my dad saw an ad in the newspaper and said to me: "Why don't you go to school to be a Superintendent?" I asked him: "What is a Superintendent?" He said: "It is like managing a hotel without food and beverage." I thought... "Interesting". I had several years of experience working in hotel administration back in Peru.

I visited the superintendent school, and met with the Principal.

There was no way I could afford $4800 for the course. She said the Government could subsidise my studies if I qualified. After applying for the grant, the school called to let me know that the government had agreed to pay for my course based on my status as a single mother and a newcomer. It was a happy moment for me and the boys!

MANIFESTING A NEW LIFE

It was a four-month course that ran from 9 to 5, five days a week. I had to learn about minor plumbing, electrical, and structural repairs, as well as administration and the Tenancy Act. This was not what I did in my hotel years, but it was okay. I was eager to learn and finished my course with the best marks! The school informed us that there was an opening for an Assistant Superintendent in a building in downtown Toronto. I went for the interview and was given the job not as an Assistant, but as the Superintendent, because of my knowledge and background. I was happy and grateful to finally have the means to remain in Canada!

In 2015, due to an unexpected "business decision" that had nothing to do with my job performance, I was laid off after 17 years of service. I was devastated! I had just turned 60 and I thought that no one would ever hire me again.

I was disillusioned. Being a fighter, I did not give in to depression. Then, I got a phone call from my friend Tania, who told me about an opportunity in the network marketing industry. I knew I would be starting over in a totally unfamiliar territory, but I also believed I had nothing to lose. I knew I wanted more control over my life, more flexibility, and have the time freedom to be around my wonderful husband and my beautiful six grandchildren.

Being laid off made me realize that there is little security in the corporate world. I gave my prior employer a large piece of my life, my entire life in Canada actually, and when decisions were made within the company, I was just a casualty. I didn't want to be in that position ever again. So I said yes to the opportunity, and began my new journey with belief and enthusiasm.

My new line of work is not easy. Rejections are common, and judgmental commentaries are sometimes harsh. Despite, it's extremely rewarding and fun! My company is backed by a multibillion-dollar brand, and is headed by a team of highly successful leaders. I have made a conscious decision to give my new career five years to achieve the level of financial success I need and want. I pursue it with energy and passion, working hard to achieve my goals.

This business has also given me the opportunity to train and mentor others as I work towards building my team. It gives me a lot of joy to be able to help them achieve their dreams of having a better life for themselves and for their families. I am striving to be a better person each and every day, educating myself and building new life-long relationships, which I cherish dearly!

MANIFESTING A NEW LIFE

Today, I am happily married to a wonderful man, Noel. I am my own boss, representing a reputable skincare company, led by two notable Stanford trained dermatologists. I am working towards leaving a legacy for my children and grandchildren, at an age when many believe their lives are entering the sunset years. Success is achieved when you help others, because it all comes back to you. There are no guarantees in life. We all need a Plan B. You can be successful no matter what your age, and even without experience in any given field. You just need to believe that anything is possible when you have a strong "why". For me, it is the legacy I will leave for my family once I am gone. What will your legacy be?

Theresia Valoczy

Theresia Valoczy is a #1 Bestselling Author, and the author of How To teach The Universal laws To Children, an International Best Selling Book. She is also certified in Indigo Studies, and is a Hypnotherapist. Theresia coaches women and young people to discover and find their passion, and to develop their personality. Her main aim is to teach people how to use their creative energy, the Universal Laws, and Angel Guidance to complete their life.

www.consciouscreatorsmag.com
www.spiritualparenting.eu

Chapter 8

Yes, I Believe! My Path of Manifestation

By Theresia Valoczy

I believe that we all have the ability of manifestating.
I believe that we are able to create our dream life.
I believe that we have the strength to become who we want to be and do what we want to do.
And this belief is the center of my life.

There was a period in my life when I did not believe this sincerely.

When my husband became ill, we had a sharp drop in revenue. We could not pay the electricity bill and our power was cut off. I could not write, I could not finish my book and the days were very tiring. During this period, I was the man and the woman, father and mother, nurse and wife in one person. Technically, my time was my own, yet I had no time to follow my dreams.

In the soul, in the spirit, and financially, I was on the edge of total collapse, unhappy, upset, and confused.

The daily joys of my few minutes of meditation led me to the herbs in my garden, where I could be alone and follow my thoughts, escape the world, and be in contact with my soul.

One day the Teraxlation method was born during a quiet meditation, born out of the negative energy of imprints covering up my ability to support the development of manifestation.

When I heard the statement "Take your heart, wrap it in love", everything changed. I realized that not only had I thought I was worthless, but I hadn't taken any responsibility for my life. I realized I was manifesting everything I was thinking about. I gave it strength. There, I gave it all my heart, embraced it, cherished it, and let all my pain and tears go away.

From that day onwards, this practice became part of my daily meditation.

Every day I sat down for a few moments and began to examine my life. I was looking for a point at which I was dissatisfied. I was looking for the cause, which had brought me to the moment. I loved the radiation of the thoughts I imagined, I put it in my hand, then firmly in my heart as I said "I love you".

MANIFESTING A NEW LIFE

And miracles began happening in my life.

By the time my husband's condition improved and he began to work again, we had become self-sufficient. We had created a small business, we surrounded ourselves with animals: dogs, cats, rabbits, chickens, goats, and bees, and we began to cultivate our land. I learned to prepare spice and tea mixtures.

Our revenue began to grow. We grew the business. I went to exhibitions with our rabbits and I studied, studied, studied.

The film *The Secret* had become my favorite and I looked up to Dr Joe Vitale. I subscribed to his newsletter, I enthusiastically read his blog posts, I drank his words, I bought his books, read, watched, listened in English and in Hungarian. I even enrolled in his courses.

It was my childhood dream to become an author.
Oh yeah!
As an adult, the sight of an international bestseller was thrilling!
I started writing in English.
I'm Hungarian and make mistakes in the English language. I said to myself 'This year my first international bestseller will appear in English'. Everyone laughed at me.

When we tell our dreams to the Universe, and wrap it in love, the doors of opportunity open.

I started my writing career.

I remember the day when someone invited me to write a chapter in her book in English. I seized the opportunity. The book became an international bestseller and the compiler who had invited me along became my good friend.

This moment played a major role in my life. It showed that despite my language difficulties, I was able to realize my dreams.

Dr Joe Vitale says: "Follow your passion".
My passion for books and writing was revived.
I continued my daily Teraxlation meditation, the realization of my dreams, and used the guidance of Doreen Virtue's Angel Daily Oracle Cards. I had three number one international bestselling books in 2016 and I started the Conscious Creators Magazine international bestseller series. Every moment was a blessing for me.

The Universe always makes way for implementation.

One of my dream was to become one of the coauthors of Dr. Joe Vitale's books. I applied his method and I put my heart into my dream, which was still only a conscious idea. I visualized it: Dr. Joe Vitale, the book, and me being in it. I repeated this vision every day.

One day, while sitting in front of my computer, I felt compelled to invite my idol to be interviewed: a short interview for my magazine's Facebook page and a longer one for the Kindle and printed version of my magazine.
I wrote him an e-mail and a response soon returned: let's go for it, let's do the interviews!
Can you imagine how I felt?
I danced around the room, jumping and shouting: 'Yes! Yes! Yes! Thank you! Thank you! Thank you!'

It was an indescribable feeling.

A month later I enrolled for his Ho 'oponopono study course.
The Teraxlation 'Take your heart' mantra combined the four Ho'oponopono phrases
'I love you. I'm sorry. Please forgive me. Thank you.'

This method was also used in preparation of the 2017 Inspirational Almanac. I wanted to work with people who are similar to me, with whom I felt a vibration, a common goal. I attracted great people into my life.

I can proudly say that one of the wildest dreams manifested itself for a Hungarian with substandard English language skills. Dr Joe Vitale became one of my coauthors of the *2017 Inspirational Almanac*!

I was now in a book with Dr. Joe Vitale!

Wonderful!

This book is the third of my Conscious Creators Book Series international bestsellers!

Every year on December 31st, I write a letter to my Past Me.

I let grievances go and I forgive my mistakes.

On January 1st, I write a letter to my Future Self, thanking it for the amazing year that I will create for me.

This year, I read last year's letter on the first of January, of which I will share a section with you:

"Dear Future Me!

I feel endless gratitude for who I am.

I feel endless gratitude for every day that I could spend with me, for the most profound silence.

I am grateful for the clarity of my internal dialogue that always points the way.

Thank you for my persistence.

Thank you for striving every day towards a better and more beautiful world.

MANIFESTING A NEW LIFE

Thank you for committing my dreams into reality. Thank you for accepting them. Thank you for accepting the possibilities with an open mind and persisting with the initiative. It seemed unrealistic, but I must take the steps to follow my heart's desire.

I am grateful for my thoughts and my actions.
It is wonderful that this year I will evoke miracles and prepare other bestseller books. It is wonderful that I appear in a book with Dr. Joe Vitale..."

WOW!
I felt Infinite Gratitude.

I believe that our dreams can come true!
I believe that they are able to create our future, our living dreams!

I live in a small town in Hungary.
I have a house, some land, and many animals.

I write, I teach, I cherish my dreams.
Dreams come true... because I make it so.

When I recognize my passion, faith and gratitude follow.
I do not insist on the how, but rather take responsibility for

my thoughts, words, feelings, and actions.
I clean myself from unwanted energies, and learn to love all the circumstances of the present.

I live on a small farm in Hungary. I am learning the English language, and there are language mistakes.
Sometimes it is difficult to express myself, I'm looking for the right words.

For a long time I thought that my success is determined by my surroundings.
It's not like this at all.
I identified my thoughts, my actions.
I dreamed of becoming an international bestselling writer.
I dreamed of creating a magazine, to be my own publisher.
I had a dream. I forgave. I let go. I cleaned my thoughts.
I worked, I learned, I weaved my dreams.

My journey is a wonderful adventure through manifestation.

MANIFESTING A NEW LIFE

BettyLou Nelson Adam

BettyLou Nelson Adam is a conservative version of the well-known Fruitcake Lady on TV giving wise candid advice to mature women. She co-authored three other books including international bestseller, "Drama Free Love". Her previous co-authored bestsellers were, "Manifesting a New Life" and "Sexy Secrets to a Juicy Love Life". They are blueprints for action for smart women to find true love. Recently married at age 72 to a wonderful man and happily living in Florida. An acclaimed university trained educator and writer who has been given Expert Writing status by a well-known publisher. Her writing is a joy to read.

Contact info:

Phone: 352-399-5929

Email: betty.adam43@gmail.com

Facebook: https://www.facebook.com/BettyNBoope

Chapter 9

Do You Realize How You Are Creating Destructive Relationship Drama?

By BettyLou Nelson Adam

Whenever we are not honoring the present moment by allowing it to be what it really is, we are creating drama by our resistance to what is in the present time. Resistance to others and to ourselves is the basis for drama. No one can even start an argument with you no matter how hard they try to get you to respond when you are in total acceptance of what is happening in the moment.

When you are living in complete and total acceptance of what is happening, that is the end of all drama in your life. We may not agree with how others live their lives or how things are happening but that does not mean we must get upset and involve ourselves in their drama. We have a responsibility to enjoy our lives and to live a peaceful existence.

When we argue with another it means we are invested in our own position and we resist what the other person is saying. As soon as opposite positions become energized, we are ready to fight to the death. We don't want to hear the other person's reasonable explanations, their needs or even try to understand them. We only want to prove we are right at the expense of precious good feelings in the relationship.

We take offense when we resist what the other person is saying, without finding out their underlying needs. The problem is our selfish position never really wins, because it is the problem in the first place. We are not seeking to truly understand the needs of the other person or their reasons for doing things. It is the difference between a debate to win and a discussion to explore options and seek solutions in a caring manner.

We can still make our position known clearly and firmly without any defensiveness or any negative attacking force behind it. When we know our needs and the needs of others and care enough to express those needs, only then can we begin to calm down and work things out.

Bad things begin to happen when we are resisting what is, without knowing the feelings and needs behind the negative messages. Drama of one kind or another will rear its ugly head in the form of conflicts, power struggles, emotional or physical violence. Violence comes from the belief that other people cause our pain and therefore deserve punishment.

Especially when we let the past or the future get in the way of the present and of what is really going on, we mix up other time frames with present time and that is how drama is made. We do that by remembering slights from the past or imagine things will not go well in the future and thereby allow that to interfere with our dealings with the other person. We must stay in present time and deal only with what is happening now.

In the heat of discussion, we may repeat, "Excuse me" with empathy until they stop and hear us. When we become defensive or angry, it is time stop and look at what is happening. Ask yourself what needs are not being met? To get them to hear us, we need to empathize with their needs so they can hear what our needs are. Specifically, we need to acknowledge the needs behind the feelings, ours as well as those of the other person.

What others say and do, may be the stimulus for, but not the cause of our feelings. When someone says something negatively, we have several options. We can blame ourselves, blame others, sense our own feelings and needs, and sense the feelings and needs hidden in the other person's negative message. Judgments, criticisms etc. are expressions of our own unmet needs and values. When others feel they are being evaluated, they feel criticized and tend to be defensive or counter attack. The more we can connect our feelings to our needs, the easier it is for others to respond compassionately. When we listen for feeling and needs, we no longer see people as monsters.

Compromise sounds good, but it does not work completely. It means both sides give something up and neither one is completely satisfied. Both sides need their needs met fully. This requires mutual concern and respect where both sides think their needs matter. They both need to realize that their own needs and the other person's well-being are mutually important. When this happens, it is amazing how quickly conflicts are resolved. Focus on what we want rather than what went wrong.

If we don't value our needs, others may not either. Emotional liberation involves stating clearly what we need in a way that communicates we are equally concerned that the needs of the other are fulfilled. Anger is a need that is not met. To get that need met we need to express our needs in a way that will be heard by the other person. To do that the other needs to know we empathize with their needs first. This is needed because people do not hear our pain when they believe they are being blamed or at fault. It is difficult but important to empathize with needs of those closest to us.

Some things we can say to find out others' feelings and needs are, "Sounds like you are feeling discouraged and you would like more support?", "I am puzzled about what you may be feeling, and wonder if you can tell me?" Or we can say, "I am sensing you are annoyed, because you need to feel more respected or appreciated? "At times, we need to guess what the other is feeling to get them talking about their feelings and needs. Try to get them to express their feelings more precisely. Women especially tend to feel that they have no right to their needs. We have been socialized to believe we are caretakers and to ignore our own needs, because we feel they are unimportant. We may have been told we are selfish for expressing our needs in the past. The fear of expressing our needs is often far worse than not expressing them. For example, a woman fearful of asking for what she needs, may fail to simply say that she has had a difficult day, is tired and wants some time in the evening to herself.

When we become aware of our own needs and the needs of others, anger gives way to understanding. To resolve and find solutions and strategies, we need to clearly express those needs to the other person in a respectful manner. Additionally, our ability to hear our own feelings and needs and empathize with them can free us from depression.

We need to express sincere appreciation to those who share their feelings, as this may be difficult for those not comfortable doing this. It is important to express that appreciation to acknowledge, not to manipulate. Complements can be judgements and are often used to manipulate others to gain favor or to get others to do what we want. It is better to say this is what you did, this is what I feel and this is the need of mine that was met.

When we are in a state of acceptance and inner peace very little can affect us. We can be loving and understanding and totally present with the other person. Sometimes a person just needs to have you present so they can express themselves and feel your comfort and support. They may not need you to solve anything. They want to feel our concern for their welfare and comfort.

In fact, we can often dissolve discord or various forms of conflict and drama without doing anything except being that peaceful presence without resisting what is being done or said. We don't have to involve ourselves in every skirmish or even take sides for that matter. Awareness of the needs of our inner body has other great benefits in the physical realm. One of them is the actual slowing down of aging in our bodies.

When the past and future no longer dominate our thinking, we do not accumulate that pain and drama and our body's cells have a greater capacity for renewal. So, if we are very aware and respectful of the needs of our inner body, our outer body will grow old at a much slower rate. And even when it does our timeless essence and peace will show through the outer form, and we won't give the impression of an old person.

Being very conscious of our body puts us at a higher spiritual force field so that anything that vibrates at a lower negative rate such as fear, anger, depression, won't enter our field of consciousness and even if it does, we don't need to offer any resistance to the drama as it will pass right through us.

Liz Smart

Liz Smart is a Life Transformation Mentor, Speaker, and Author. She reads and works within your energy field to release the emotional blockages that keep you from enjoying total wellness. Using her intuitive savant side, 25 years of studies in metaphysical philosophies, and her 20-year background as a health facilitator in naturopathy, Liz will guide you on how you can balance your spiritual, emotional, and physical health.

Her greatest passion is being a devoted homeschooling mother of two. Along with her mentoring program, Liz hosts travelling retreats. She lives her passion in reminding you, YOU are Powerful and Adored.

You can reach Liz Smart:

Website: www.lizsmart.com

Email: liz@lizsmart.com

Facebook https://www.facebook.com/liz.lizsmart

Chapter 10

Everything is as it Should be. All is Well. Life is Good.

By Liz Smart

I would like to share with you a little of what has gone on in my life over the past few years, not for pity or to wallow in it. I am sharing my story in hopes of inspiring you. My mission in life has become crystal clear from having lived through these challenges.

A few years ago, my husband was audited due to a business decision gone bad. After two years of going back and forth with the government we filed a joint petition bankruptcy in early November 2014, losing everything we had built over 20 years. My husband had a hard time getting past this, associating it with him having failed us. After the initial range of emotions over the audit, I chose to see it as an opportunity for us to start over. After all, we had our health, and I believe our health is our wealth. We were told most marriages do not survive the stress of bankruptcy. Ironically, we experienced some of our closest bond during this time after having lived a few rock and roll years. I had been wanting to downsize, being a fan of the tiny house nation, and the material world was much less appealing to me by now. All I wanted to do was simplify our lives and travel.

In the summer of 2014, we had made an agreement to stay together on the promise that in November, we would take part in a conference together that focused on personal development, finances, and relationships. I wanted to make sure we did not fall back into the same trap. At the last minute, my husband backed out and I attended it alone.

Upon my return, we agreed to separate. We experienced a very successful, mutually respectful, loving separation. We enjoyed Christmas together and our relationship seemed to take a new positive direction. We were getting into the swing of this new agreement; my business was flourishing and I travelled with my daughters on a business/pleasure trip. Life was good.

Then, 5 days after our return, in March of 2015, while staying with us, my husband appeared unwell. I took him to the hospital. He was experiencing a massive heart attack and we found out later that it appeared he had suffered several more over the past week. To everyone's amazement, he had survived.

MANIFESTING A NEW LIFE

The year that followed had to be one of the most emotionally painful we had ever experienced. I put everything on hold. I was tending to my husband while trying my best to keep the children's needs met as well. In and out of hospital for months. Since we were self-employed with no group insurance, and having just declared bankruptcy we were barely able to hang on to our home. We had to step on our pride and go to a food bank. That was tough, I never thought I would have to do that. I mean we had fallen so hard. It was a very humiliating and humbling experience. Somehow though, I knew this experience would serve me. Even then, I could see the bigger picture. It sure helped me let go of layers of keeping up appearances. Even though we were in survival mode, I knew it would eventually pass and that it would serve a higher purpose.

In September 2015, I took on a part time job and even though we had many more challenges throughout the year, we managed to keep our home and started buying groceries again.

In January 2016, I travelled to Texas on business and served on the crew at an event and began mentoring clients once more. Things looked hopeful.

Compiled by **PATRICIA LEBLANC**

Then on March 4th, 2016, 2 days after the Doctor told me she believed he had another year or two to live, Jerry passed away suddenly and peacefully in his sleep at the hospital.

I always knew I would be a young widow. Knowing, mentally preparing, and being, are much different. We went through many contrasts in our 20-year marriage, but we always had a deep love for one another. I must say, I have never felt his love greater than I do now that he is on the other side of the veil.
When the Doctor called at 5:30 am that day, all she said was that he was not doing well and that I should come to the hospital immediately, but Jerry had already woken me up 30 minutes earlier, in a dream. I knew I would find him having already passed. I stayed by his side for hours, counting my blessings that we had had deep conversations about him choosing love and happiness over fear and anger. I was beyond grateful that he had passed in a state of peace, joy and love.

Without life insurance and with me trying to cut costs, I made a most ridiculously bad decision: to cancel our home insurance just months prior to his heart attack. I also needed to pay the equity back from our home from the bankruptcy. I had one year to prepare myself for this psychologically, however the blow of it was still hard to swallow. At least we had prepared a will when the children were born. But still, I was barely getting back on my feet, financially. I didn't have the money to bury him and this overshadowed my grieving. Thankfully, I was able to borrow some money from my sister Ann to cover the arrangements until the government death benefit came in. I did my due diligence to prepare a funeral by means of contacting all the wholesalers from the industry, and no one was the wiser. We had a beautiful life celebration for Jerry and I believe it was pulled off with style.

As I sit here writing, it has not yet hit the one-year mark. I have lived all the emotions you can imagine when loosing a spouse. I have moments where unexpectedly, tears come without notice. That being said, I have found so many blessings. I have been able to step away and see the bigger picture.

If there were life insurance, perhaps I would be travelling the world hanging out on the beaches losing track of time right now. I still plan to travel the world and hang out on the beach, however, I will be doing so while sharing my message. This contrast I have gone through has pushed me to step up my game at a much larger scale then I could have imagined. Everything is as it should be. All is well. Life is good.

Jerry continues to be a great teacher from beyond. We have shared many conversations since his passing. The missing piece finally came together. It has changed the way I mentor my clients. I have fully embraced my intuitive savant side into my practice.

So much wonderment has come into our lives.

In November 2016, I applied and was accepted to be part of an amazing event in Florida. I took my daughters along with me for 3 weeks without fully knowing how we would pull it off. We found ourselves living in abundance. Serendipities had come into play once we had unleashed the magic. Then, in December, I took part in a highly successful Spiritual and Metaphysical show where I offered my mentoring package along with non-stop intuitive readings from 10am to 7pm, while my daughters showcased some of their own artwork and homemade goodies. They kept asking me how come I was making all these people cry. Tears of joy they were, tears of joy. Connected to spirit, living my bliss. It was a life changing experience. Fully embracing and embodying all of it. Sharing my story as a guest speaker at events enhanced my mentoring program, as well as my workshops. I am extremely excited about this upcoming year, with the retreats I will be hosting, the books I will be writing and compiling, and the life changing adventure being created and all that is awaiting in the future.

I trust my story has indeed inspired you. My mission is to help remind you, YOU are Powerful and Adored. Realize what a blessing life is, live to the fullest, and choose love over fear.
This is my wish for all. Much love to you. Big Hugs xxx

MANIFESTING A NEW LIFE

Short Manifesting Story #2

That Time I Manifested a new Course

By Twyla Clarke

It was July 2016 and I had just finished watching *I am not your Guru!* I remember being so moved during the movie and crying with each story. While watching I declared to myself that I would do whatever it took to get my coaching business off the ground. I decided to follow whatever signs appeared without question.

The next day I logged into Facebook and scrolled my timeline as I often do. I came across an ad from a seven-figure coach, who I was friends with, but had stopped showing up in my feed. I read the ad and immediately felt like this was the sign. I thought "Wow, that was quick!" I joined the challenge and began to connect with all these wonderful ladies. When the challenge started I knew I was going all in, I was going to complete all five days with everything in me.

Day one was released and I did it. It was a stretch, but I got it done. Day two came, same thing, I could feel myself growing into this woman. The challenge was amazing! That day I saw a post about winning a spot in the course that would be launched after the challenge. What? How did I miss this? Could I be one of the people to win a spot? There were a lot of women in the group and they were each giving it their all!

Day three, I was in; there was no mistake that I found that ad. I didn't even think about winning anymore, there were so many women in the group. My goal was to be in the vortex of these women, to learn as much as I could from this challenge. I knew I wouldn't be able to afford the course. I had lost my job, my coaching business wasn't where I wanted it to be, and, to top things off, my baby was just a few months old. Day four and day five were two of the hardest and challenging days. After all, this was a challenge. I kept going, kept connecting, read and listened to as many of the other ladies as I could. If nothing else I wanted to at least support everyone else on this journey with me.

The challenge finished and somewhere, deep down I felt the lure of this course and wondered could it be me? Could I be one of the lucky three to win? To have these two phenomenal women in my back pocket, learning and picking their brain. I pushed the thoughts aside, but secretly I felt it calling me.

The announcement came. I had won third place. I didn't care about coming in first or second, third meant winning the program. It was one of the most amazing days I've ever experienced. I screamed, I cried, but most of all I was extremely thankful!

Julie Bourbeau

Julie Bourbeau is a language expert. She helps businesses and charitable organizations translate and proofread their material, so they can reach out to a broader market. Julie helps her clients achieve presence, keep their message consistent and look professional.

Julie is a heart and soul, free-spirited and determined entrepreneur. She is the founder of Julie Bourbeau, Translation Services which grew out of her desire and commitment to being a stay at home mom to both her kids. She has now grown it into a full-time business and a team of 4 collaborators.

You can learn more about Julie by:

Facebook:
https://www.facebook.com/JulieBourbeauServicesdetraductio n/

Linkedin https://ca.linkedin.com/in/julie-bourbeau-2483b114

Signing up for her newsletter here http://eepurl.com/cakMY1

Chapter 11

Freedom and Responsibility

By Julie Bourbeau

From as far back as I can remember, I always knew I could make things happen. I always wanted to do whatever I wanted to do, and I've always had massive determination. As a child, I remember not understanding limits. I didn't understand why I wasn't allowed to do certain things, to say certain things or to question authority. I grew up wanting to do more, to be more, to be allowed to do more, and I couldn't understand why my mom would not let me ... after all, I was 10 years old!

Although my mom set limits for my sister and I, she raised us to believe that we were responsible for our own happiness and our own life. I can still hear her saying: "Only you can make yourself happy. Don't wait for any one to do that for you!" So, I grew up knowing that if I wanted good things to happen I had to make the right choices, and with that came the consequences of having bad things happen when I made the wrong choices. I didn't like that too much. Despite, I still chose to make the wrong choices.

In my late teens and early twenties, I became a pro at avoiding all responsibility for my life. I became an expert at blaming people and thereby giving them power over my life and my happiness. If a guy didn't like me, it was the end of the world. If a guy broke up with me because I was too wild (which happened more than once), it was the end of the world. I wanted to be happy and to be free, but to me this meant zero responsibility. Acting upon my beliefs, I did just that. I spent my college and university years partying, abusing drugs and alcohol and living in a way I thought meant being "free". I was in school because I loved being in school, but didn't put any effort into it. I graduated college by the skin of my teeth and later quit university, because my artificial freedom got me into such a state of psychosis that I could no longer function.

I hit bottom in 1992, at the age of 23. At that time, I wished I could have made excuses as to why I ended up in this state. I wished I could have blamed someone for what was happening to me, but I couldn't. I suffered from the disease of addiction. My own choices brought me to where I was and I only had two choices left: either I kept on abusing substances and sink even further or I sought help. Either choice was my responsibility. The fact that I suffer from this disease, which I believe is a mental illness, is not my fault. However, what I do about it is my responsibility! No one else could get sober for me and I couldn't do it for anyone other than for myself.

MANIFESTING A NEW LIFE

I decided to seek recovery. I made a decision to trust some type of God I didn't understand, I cleaned house (a pretty way of saying I dealt with @?%&) and eventually began to help others.

I felt that I was given a new lease on life, but I didn't feel that my circumstances were getting better fast enough for me. I was full of fear, I was uncertain about what I wanted to do with my life and I didn't feel like I was living up to my full potential. I wanted it all, I wanted it now, but I didn't know what I wanted.

One night, in February of 1999, as I was about to fall asleep, I heard a voice – yes, a voice – telling me: "You are going to go back to university!" To this day, I have no clue where that voice came from, but the desire was planted and began to nag at me.

Three days later, I was let go from a job that I truly was not suited for. I remember telling my boss: "I am not saying that to be rude, but you have done me the biggest favour. I am going back to school."

A few days later, I turned to my friend Jacques for validation and inspiration. Jacques was in his early 50s and had just graduated from university. He asked me: "If you go back to school, how old would you be when you graduate?" "33" I said. His advice was "You can be 33 with a degree or you can be 33 without a degree, but you'll still be 33." So, three years later, at the age of 33, I graduated from university with honours.

In their book "Ask and It Is Given", Esther and Jerry Hicks (The Teachings of Abraham) state, *"There is never a reason for you to be without something you desire. Nor is there ever a reason for you to experience something that you do not desire - for you hold absolute control of your experiences."* (p. 125). I have come to believe that if God, Source, the Universe, Higher Power, call it what you may, plants a desire in me, it is because I have in me what it takes to fulfill it. If not, what would be the point?

My experience and my journey have both taught me that I can achieve whatever I desire. I don't believe that the Law of Attraction is about me wishfully thinking my way through life and waiting for my desires to manifest. I believe rather, that if I am facing the direction of my desires and dreams, and just do the next right thing in that direction, I will get there. If I am looking in the past, focussing on my resentments, blaming others for what "they" did to me, I am facing an opposite direction and totally losing sight of my goals. I can't go north if I keep driving south.

MANIFESTING A NEW LIFE

I am also a firm believer that whatever is worth having is worth working for and, most of all, planning for. I am not talking about blood, sweat and tears here. I am talking about doing things differently - smarter.

I started my own business 10 ½ years ago, while on maternity leave. I couldn't see myself working for someone else anymore and I felt the only way to live up to my potential was to create the job I wanted! I became a single mom 3 years later and, although times were rough financially and emotionally, I never gave up on my business or myself. My business became about survival and was a means to my end of wanting to be home with my kids. Now that both kids are in school full time, it's about my desire to serve others, sharing my gifts, attracting like-minded clients (which I do) and, most of all, freedom. I can't build my business waiting for people to call me. I can have all the faith I want, if I don't put myself out there, if I don't get out of the house to network and meet with people, if I don't set goals and deadlines and if I don't keep in touch with prospects and clients, my business will not survive and I will not thrive. I can pray all I want for success and abundance to manifest themselves in my life, if I sit home and watch television and get sucked in by the news and what's going on in the world, instead of participating fully in my life, nothing will change.

These days, I'm in a warrior mode. Not in the sense of fighting everything and everyone, but in facing my fears and smashing those beliefs I feel I have been brainwashed to believe and to adopt from society, mass media and generations and generations of limited beliefs about success. I feel that, as humans, we have been programmed to live in the status quo, to resist change and to do just what we need to do to survive – no more. We strive for perfection while we give up on our vision, because of competition and striving for perfection by comparison. Personally, I don't have a desire to compete and I don't want to be perfect (less and less, anyway), yet I believe that I am deserving of success, in all areas of my life. My experience has taught me that there is enough wealth, joy, peace, love and all those good things to go around. I am totally entitled to my share even though the media, especially in the news, is telling me that the world is an awful place to live. My focus in on creating that same wealth, joy, peace and love, and all those good things while sharing it with others. I wish all these things for you too, and more!

MANIFESTING A NEW LIFE

Tamie M Joyce

Tamie M is a professional online marketer who has a passion for inspiring others to step into their power and set themselves free. Freedom is her core value. Psychological, emotional, spiritual, time and money freedom all come together to create personal freedom for the individual. As an online entrepreneur, she inspires others to create the lives of their dreams through personal development and business building strategies. She coaches others in developing their mindset and their skills so they can leverage the internet to build businesses, enabling people to live the laptop lifestyle and work from anywhere on the planet, provided they have a laptop, a cell phone and an internet connection.

You can learn more about Tamie M at: www.TamieM.com
Follow her on Facebook at: www.facebook.com/tamiem.biz/
You can contact Tamie M by email at:
tamiemjoyce@gmail.com

Chapter 12

Stop Running from Your Pain

Tamie M Joyce

Ever since I was a little girl I dreamt of finding my King, that one true love to be deeply connected to, walk off into the sunset with, living happily ever after. You know... the stuff fairy tales are made of! Little did I know that I would have many internal mountains to climb before I would be ready to attract the kind of true, lasting and deep love I had been dreaming of.

You see, from an early age, I believed I was unworthy, unlovable, that there was something inherently wrong with me. And when that is your fundamental belief, it is very difficult to attract honest, sincere, genuine, authentic, and healthy love. It wasn't until I was in my late 30's when I really began to understand that if you do not love yourself, attracting the kind of healthy love I had been longing for is impossible.

I was born to two very young adult children of alcoholism. They grew up in poverty, violence and in my opinion, were deeply affected by the mental and spiritual illnesses that plagued the family dynamics in each of their lives. I was not planned, and as I understood it in my young mind growing up, I had been a mistake. Needless to say, these two young people did not have the skills to make a marriage work, let alone raise a child for that matter. By the time I was a toddler my mother disappeared from my life entirely. My father handed me off to his mother and was for the most part absent and preoccupied with his own alcoholism and the chaos of his life. When he was around, his influence was far from positive. My grandmother, who had spent twenty-five years of her life being brutally beaten by my alcoholic grandfather, took on the task of raising me on her small welfare check, with no contribution from either of my parents. She did the best she could with the limited resources she had, and in many respects, she did a good job. But she had her own issues. Uneducated and poor, she had not dealt with the trauma she suffered all of those years in any real way. So I was raised by a woman who herself was in a tremendous amount of pain. For all of her great qualities, and there were many, her tendency was to manipulate and control me through guilt and shame.

During those young years, I was made to feel unworthy and unlovable in more ways than most people can imagine. My mother's disappearing act was never discussed. I had no idea why she left and clearly wanted nothing to do with me. My father was as I said, preoccupied. There were aunts and uncles as well as a stepmother who all had major unresolved issues, which manifested in my experience as little to no boundaries with or compassion for a child who nobody really seemed to want around. My grandmother's low self-esteem and need for approval from family members and relatives meant that there was very little in the way of boundaries and protection for me as a child. This resulted in numerous painful abandonment experiences, emotional, psychological, verbal, physical and sexual abuse. I felt unwanted, rejected, and wrong for just being in existence.

Basically, I grew up in a very sick family system surrounded by unrecovered adult children of alcoholism, raging codependents, active alcoholics, narcissists and a pedophile uncle who is such a master manipulator that he is the last person in the family anyone would ever suspect of such diabolical behavior. And that was just our immediate family. Then there was the extended family and relatives. Some of the most judgmental, critical, shame-based, compassionless people you'd ever like to meet. Not a single champion to be found.

Abandoned by my parents, disliked, unwanted, mistreated and often abused by family members, sexually molested and manipulated into silence by a trusted uncle, suffice to say I did not grow up with any level of self-esteem or understanding of the concept of self-love. Hurt people hurt people and I grew up surrounded by some seriously hurt people. And thus began my journey.

As a result, I myself started drinking alcoholically at the age of thirteen. I was a runaway and a ward of the court by the time I was fourteen. By sixteen I found my way back into my grandmother's home and continued my journey of self-destructive behavior all the while seeking to find the love I had been craving my whole life outside of myself.

From sixteen into my mid-thirties I had a series of romantic relationships. Many of them were short-lived and for the most part ending in painful disaster. What I did not understand all of those years was that until I was willing to surrender and face the pain I had been running from my entire life, to examine, accept and heal the wounds, I could only attract what was a match to what I had been carrying. I could only repeat the patterns ingrained in my subconscious mind long before I had any say in the matter. I could only attract what I was; unhealthy, wounded, toxic, pain.

After years of spinning my wheels in the same patterns, at the age of thirty-six, I finally found my way into recovery. It was a major turning point. With the exception of some dry periods, I had been self-medicating for more than two decades, and try as I may my life was in a perpetual state of unmanageability. In spite of an abundance of potential and opportunity, I could never quite figure out how to get and how to keep my life 'together'. Recovery was without a doubt the best thing that could have happened to me.

Over a decade later I can tell you that putting the cork in the bottle was just the beginning. The real recovery work began when I became willing to face and deal with my family of origin issues... and the wounds were deep. It was a long, uncomfortable road that involved twelve step recovery, a lot of individual therapy, participation in group therapy and intensive treatment specifically designed for people affected by the family disease of alcoholism, as well as many other forms of healing, information and education that have all contributed to the slow but sure healing process. My recovery journey was and continues to be all about finding my way back to the real me and learning to love and accept myself at my core, flaws and all, in the deepest possible way. To say that the journey has been worthwhile would be a colossal understatement.

For the record, I spent the better part of eight years single while I worked on myself. Occasionally dipping my toe back into the dating arena, each time seeing with clarity by what I was attracting and what I was attracted to, that I still had work to do. So it would be back to the single-minded focus of healing myself.

At the age of 45, I finally met the one! The one man I had dreamt of finding my entire life. He was worth the work and worth the wait. Today, I am blissfully in love with the man of my dreams. Every day without fail, he treats me the way I first needed to learn to treat myself... with gentle kindness, compassion, understanding, respect and genuine healthy love. He is my barometer for how far I have come. I know I have healed deeply, having been able to attract the quality of Man that I now have in my life.

Here's what I've learned...

No matter how much we study the Law of Attraction and mentally project our hopes, wishes, dreams, and desires, it is what is going on in the deeper levels of our being, our subconscious that really counts and truly attracts. Our outside is always a reflection of our inside. Not just our conscious thoughts. That's only 5% of the game. The other 95% dwells in our subconscious, the stuff we spend our lives trying to avoid, run and hide from. Until we become willing to stop medicating ourselves, whether that be with food, alcohol, drugs, excessive shopping, work, sex, gambling or any other means of distraction, the universe, by virtue of the Law of Attraction, is going to continue to bring to us the people, situations and circumstances that call our attention to what remains unhealed within ourselves. We cannot put ice cream on top of poop and expect positive results. Believe me... I tried for many years. It does not work.

We must be willing to feel it in order to heal it. We must be willing to heal in order to be able to attract and manifest the best that the universe has in store for us. Trust me when I tell you the journey is worth it!

Compiled by **PATRICIA LEBLANC**

Paula Johnson, M.A.

Paula Johnson is a helper, healer, mentor and author who gets
fired up guiding women in creating financial success and live
abundant lives. Paula empowers women by helping them
make peace with their money, connect with their intuition,
gifts, and purpose, break through their existing money blocks,
so they can manifest their most amazing life. With a Master's
Degree in Counselling Psychology, Paula knows how to help
people get to the heart of issues that blocks them from
manifesting what they truly desire. Drawing on her own
journey of healing and 25 years of personal development,
spiritual teachings, education, and knowledge, Paula is
dedicated to helping people make those quantum
breakthroughs in their money, life and business. Paula
intertwines practical and spiritual practices that have inspired,
motivated, and empowered thousands of people to take steps
into their GREATNESS and cultivate a successful life.

Website: pauladjohnson.com
Facebook: Paula Johnson worldwide
https://www.facebook.com/paulajohnsoncounselling/
Facebook: Paula Johnson
https://www.facebook.com/paula.johnson.984349

Chapter 13

Living My Yoga: Lessons on and off the mat to Manifest a Meaningful Life

By Paula Johnson, M.A.

When I started yoga more than 16 years ago, I didn't know what a profound impact it would have on my life. The first class I attended was a Kundalini community class. At the end, we did savasana, and I was hooked. I had a one-year-old baby at the time and to think that I could lay in peace, without distraction, was heavenly. That was the beginning of my journey of self-discovery, acceptance and love.

Today, I share the lessons yoga taught me. This practice awoke something inside and invited me daily to step up, show up and manifest a more meaningful life. When I learned how to practice yoga, I learned how to practice life.

Loving My Body

When I began practicing hot yoga I was intimidated and self-conscious. I wasn't the most flexible person in the room nor the most elegant. It was so damn hot and humid that, at first, I found it almost unbearable. I went to the back of the room, because I saw my body as weak and inflexible. When things got tough I just wanted to leave.

In that room, full of large mirrors, I had to look at my whole body. At first, I didn't like what I saw. I was overweight and out-of-shape. Mirror, mirror on the wall who is the ugliest of them all? ME.

Slowly, I began to turn my focus within, away from the room and the mirrors and the heat. It became clear that I wouldn't find peace in that room if I didn't first find it within myself. This was the first, most important step on my journey back to self-compassion. I began to unconditionally accept all of my parts, learning to love myself from the inside out. I rewrote the story I held about myself, and as my body grew stronger, so did my mind. As I became stronger, flexible, and physically fit, I felt better. When I felt better, I ate better, and I dropped more than 25 pounds. I felt the strongest, fittest, and happiest I had felt in all my life.

Looking into the Eyes of the Teacher

Growing my self-love taught me to be my own teacher. Each day I looked into my eyes in the mirrors. As I learned to practice the poses that were outside my comfort zone, my love and appreciation for my body grew, and I began to experience a deep sense of self-trust.

MANIFESTING A NEW LIFE

In the past, I would get caught in internal wars about making the 'right' decisions. I could rationalize why I "should do this" or "shouldn't do that." I agonized about making the wrong decisions. I would look outside myself for answers and reassurance.

Most of my life I lived in indecisiveness. Being my own teacher in the yoga room, I became the CEO of my body and mind. At first, my mind told me the poses were too hard, I needed to back off, or that it wasn't good for me, creating tension between my mind and body. I learned to find ease in the effort of each pose, which translated into trusting that I could handle it. It seems very strange to reflect back and recognize how much anxiety was caused by my lack of self-confidence.

As harmony between my mind and body grew, something else started to happen. I could hear my own internal voice, my own intuition and inspiration. I had new ideas, new possibilities, and I felt motivated. That battle within retreated. I cultivated a strong relationship with the divine universe. As my intuition grew, I differentiated between my ego (fear) and my higher self.

I began to trust my choices, my decision-making process, and I stepped into my power of trusting my next step. Did that mean that everything has worked out exactly the way I envisioned? No! But I did, and do, believe in myself. I now embrace uncertainty and trust my decisions. This lesson has been instrumental in developing my manifesting abilities.

Breath – something so natural has such a profound impact on our lives! Yoga taught me a lot about breath control, and how it can be used to calm the mind and body. I learned that I could inhale peace and exhale tension. My breath taught me to stay in my body and not to run from my sensations, emotions, and uncomfortable feelings, even in challenging poses.

I clearly remember the first time I used breath control to manage my body and mind. I had just done a heart-opening pose called Camel. After the deep backbend, we lay in savasana, which should be calming, but my heart was beating fast and I felt myself go into panic. All I could think is, "I might be dying, the room is too hot, this isn't good for me, I can't breathe!"

Then a breakthrough happened. I came back to my breath and spontaneously I said, "I am safe, look around, I am in savasana." It was like a fever broke and the anxiety melted away. It was in that moment that I broke an emotional pattern I had held for over 30 years, one that let fear and anxiety rule my life. I learned that day that my feelings and emotions do not define me. I could choose my feelings and cultivate feelings of peace. This unlocked my ability to stop my stress response from taking over in difficult situations. I could take a breath and sit with my emotions and not have to flee or fight. This knowledge reassures me that I can use my breath to connect to that sense of peace, no matter where I am.

Intention

Without intention, my focus can spill in many directions, leaving me overwhelmed, frustrated and even angry. Intention is a powerful tool that guides me and directs me. When I am on the mat, I may practice the intention of presence in my body and my breath. When my critical mind starts or I find myself 'futurizing', I breathe, come back to my intention and my body. Off the mat the same process holds true: without intention, life becomes just another task that I cannot control. Setting intentions helps me take responsibility for my own ability to create what I want, while not falling victim to life's circumstances. The power of intention translates to bringing awareness, focus and energy to the things I want to cultivate in my practice and in my life.

Quiet my mind, open my heart

Yoga is seen as a place to cultivate peace and a zen-like nature. Bullshit! This was a difficult assumption to let go of. Quiet my mind? Easier said than done. The more challenging the poses, the more my mind complained.

In class our teacher would say don't let that "monkey mind" take over. My monkey mind was so loud, it was my ruler, it was my controller, it was my boss. It had all kinds of nasty things to say to me. It was critical, full of hatred and self-loathing. It lived in my subconscious, every day controlling me. I got so used to it that sadly, it was my norm. It would tell me all kinds of hateful things:

"You are not smart enough."
"You are not good enough,"
"You can't do that.
"Nobody cares about that."
" You should have planned better."

It was a never-ending stream of criticism. I had no idea how much power it had over me until I started yoga. For a long time, I believed being self-critical was what motivated me, kept me humble, modest and good. But what it really did was keep me small, weak, scared, and wounded. It made me believe I didn't have a lot to contribute.

The connection between quieting my mind and opening my heart came deep within the poses. In the full expression of poses, I could connect with my true self. Each class I was instructed to find the full expression of the pose and to breathe into the resistance. I was instructed to be aware of my mind chatter, but not become it. Through that repetition of practice and intention, I broke through my constant self-criticism to find a new story, a new view of myself. I began to recognize and believe that I am smart, worthy and deserving. I believed it and I felt it within. I spoke to myself with kindness, and learned to be receptive to self-compassion and self-love. I now approach life with a lighter, loving and open heart, cheering myself on, and in turn mirroring that to others.

Yoga is the vehicle I used for my journey back to self-love and to manifesting my amazing life. I have learned to call peace and love into my consciousness. This consistent practice of focusing, getting back on track, connecting to self, and the flow between effort and ease, can become the very light that guides you (home) OM!

Namaste!

Carol-Chantal Séguin

Carol-Chantal Séguin is the Founder & President of WOW-World-of-Women Social Network Inc.

For the past 30 years, Carol's passion in finance and accounting has made her a suitable business coach for Women Entrepreneurs. Through her own development as an entrepreneur and with a vast amount of business experience, Carol has established herself as a reputable business leader.
Carol understands the difficulties, as well as the pleasures of running a business and is eager to share her experiences with other women. She believes in commerce, philanthropy and helping other women find their own path to success. By providing women with the right tools and information, Carol is certain they will find success through informed decisions about their future endeavours.

You can connect with Carol-Chantal Séguin
http://wow-world-of-women.com
https://www.facebook.com/carolchantal.seguin
https://www.facebook.com/WorldOfWomenNetwork/

Chapter 14

WOW – World-of-Women

By Carol Chantal Séguin

In June 2012, I founded WOW – World-of-Women, in the greater Montreal area. While I was mentoring 3 women entrepreneurs with their businesses, we had a coffee date at a local Tim Hortons and discussed creating a community of "Women Helping Women". We strategized and came up with why, and how we would do that by creating a Social Network for Women Entrepreneur. Everyone said "WOW" at the same time. As I scribbled it behind a paper place mat, I knew it was going to be the start of a great community of World-of-Women. It has since expanded across Quebec & Ontario in cities such as Ottawa, Montreal, Kingston, South & North shores of the Montreal area and Prescott Russell counties (with plans to go across Canada & the USA).

The expansion of the WOW network is a testament to its effectiveness! Women love connecting in their communities and working towards a better and stronger future both for themselves and their fellow WOW Ambassadors/members.

When I started this group on Meetup I didn't know how to grow it until I decided to invest into our very own website (www.WOW-World-of-Women.com) and I added a Facebook page to connect with other cities, because I wanted to provide women with an opportunity to network, socialize and grow their businesses.

Together, the WOW Women support one another, making new connections and create new friendships for a better community of Women helping Women in times of success and defeat.

The mission of WOW is to mentor, support, help, promote and encourage our Women Entrepreneurs. We value our WOW Ambassadors and support one another in a positive, encouraging way. We hold various workshops that help out ambassadors to start, grow, and manage their businesses. We also hold financial information sessions, with marketing as well as numerous networking events & showcase our Ambassadors monthly. We choose different venues to compliment and promote them and we accommodate every type of business, service, product, manufacturer, professional, self-employed and consultants in a variety of fields.

MANIFESTING A NEW LIFE

We are hoping that Women across Canada will be connecting in their communities and working towards a better and stronger future both for themselves and for their fellow Ambassadors/members.

WOW – World-of-Women encourages new business owners and those thinking of starting a business, to reach out to the WOW community to connect with other like-minded women. By working together, we can make a tremendous difference in the success of any business. By "all playing in the same sandbox" without competition, we can learn how to collaborate together!

When I moved back home to Ottawa in 2015 to be the primary caregiver to my 82-year-old mother who was recovering from brain surgery and a subsequent stroke, the only thing that gave me a break from my daily routine was WOW Ambassador activities.

They kept me in a positive mood and inspired me to continue with the motto/vision/growth of the "Women helping Women" community.

Always driven to help others achieve business success, my philosophy is: together we can accomplish so much more, by learning, supporting and encouraging each other.

Another "Aha moment" came at a WOW POP up Shop vendor show where I suggested to the two ladies representing the same product (competitors), that they should combine their tables to make one bigger, more attractive display. We need to learn to "play in the same sandbox". Their booth had the most client engagement that day! Both were surprised how fun and easy it is to combine, collaborate and make new friends with common goals that they could share their knowledge in a collaborative and supporting way instead being by themselves and struggle. Playing in the same sand box is more fun... than throwing sand at each other.

I love motivating, inspiring and mentoring entrepreneurs. "Every day I am blessed to be surrounded by amazing women! As much as I hope to inspire these women, they have likewise inspired me."

I have learned to manifest a new life! Had I not moved to Ottawa and started other chapters of WOW World-of-Women, maybe WOW would not have been in both provinces and would not have continued to grow every day! I am forever grateful to all the women whom I have met along the way and who are now part of a growing community of Women helping Women and are following their dreams like I did!

WOW for now…

MANIFESTING A NEW LIFE

Valentina Gjorgjievska

Valentina Gjorgjievska had a successful career in the Community Services industry before becoming a writer. She has assisted many people to overcome their barriers during this time as well as assist them to re-enter the workforce. Valentina is also currently working with people with disabilities and severe mental health issues nationwide across Australia. In addition to this, Valentina became an International Best Selling Author with the release of Living Without Limitations: 30 Stories to Heal Your World and Family Ties: What Binds Us and Tears Us Apart. Valentina has a creative flair with a passion for music, reading, novel writing. She sang professionally in her younger years.

Facebook: @valentinag23

Chapter 15

Acquire That Dream Job

By Valentina Gjorgjievska

From the time I was a teenager, I always knew that I wanted to help people. I had a compassionate soul that was bursting at the seams and that is still a big part of me today. My High School Career Counsellor however, kept discouraging me to follow the career path that I desired and tried to steer me in the direction of Commerce at University, which I initially did follow against my wishes. I didn't end up finishing that degree and I found myself in my early 20s, searching for a job that would allow me to help people. I didn't find it initially, having no work experience except for a retail job that I sustained for 5 years during my time at school. I had to start right at the bottom and work my way up. The first job came through a family friend who decided to give me work experience for 3 weeks as a receptionist. They found I was picking it up so fast that they decided to put me on the books until I found the job that I was looking for. The next job was just the next step as it was more work as a receptionist just in a different environment, but it wasn't helping people.

It wasn't until the third job, a few years later, that I finally struck gold, landing myself with my previous experience, another reception job. This time in the employment services industry. It was a foot in the door for the start of my helping people journey. The manager gave the initial administration job that I applied for to a more experienced candidate, but gave me a reception job that was not advertised.

The rest is history.

That was ten years ago in 2007. Ten years later, I'm at the top of the game, still helping people, except now it's not just in one small location. It's now across the country. So where am I going with all of this?

At any stage of your life you may find yourself looking for that dream job and in some cases, just finding a job. It doesn't matter if it's your dream job, just as long as you're employed. However, most people find it easier said than done. Application after application is sent off, although nothing comes through, not even one interview. 'Why is this?' I hear from people in frustration. It could be many things. There is the concern of not having enough experience or having the right qualifications, and being the right fit for the job. The one thing that you must have regardless of what job you're trying to obtain, is a positive mindset, because you will be rejected; many times.

MANIFESTING A NEW LIFE

So how do you obtain that dream job whatever that may be? Firstly, you need to research the industry that you want to work in. If you just finished your diploma or degree, chances are the employer is also looking for work experience. In order to increase your chances in being successful, take up that intern job or do voluntary work for a few weeks in a business that could give you the necessary skills you need. The other thing that doesn't automatically come to mind is do what I did: start from the bottom and work your way up. In my time as an employment consultant, not many people were willing to do this, although it is something that will definitely get you to where you want to be. Take that entry-level job! You might be trained by the company internally. With that positive mindset, you never know. Within months you could be climbing up the ladder to be that Marketing Manager that you always wanted to be. It has happened!

There is also the issue that you are already working, but not in your dream job. You've been working as a sales clerk for 5 years, but it just doesn't make you happy anymore. This can be a little daunting as time can be scarce with your work hours and family commitments. Find that spare time where you can quickly fit in research on how to get into the industry, how to obtain that work experience or what qualifications you need and how you're going to complete them if you don't have them already. Find that time either when you put the children to bed, while waiting for your other half to come home from work, or when your mother is pressuring you to clean the house at certain times during the day. It will take time, as the moments you have to dedicate to this are just small patches here and there.

Your potential future employer will be looking for something in particular, and you need to understand what that is to determine if you have it in order to be successful in obtaining the job. A lot of people complete a degree and expect to land a job immediately, although in today's market this is becoming rare. In order to understand what the employer is looking for, you must do some research on the job that you're applying for. There is also the trick of tapping into the hidden job market.

The hidden job market makes up the majority of the percentage of jobs obtained, although the reason they are hidden is because you won't find them advertised online or in any newspaper. They are created specifically for you once the employer is aware of you and your skill set. This is where your marketing skills come in, a task that most people are uncomfortable with. To tap in to the hidden job market, you need to cold canvass yourself to employers, network at social events and through friends. Also, send out your resume to the HR department of the company and sell yourself without specifying on the application for a particular job.

MANIFESTING A NEW LIFE

Start by creating a list of companies that you could potentially contact in the industry that you are trying to get into from the research that you initially conducted. Once you have this list, then you can either cold canvass via phone or send the application through the post – address it to the attention of the HR department of the company that you are sending it to. Make sure that you have an up to date resume. If you've worked for a very long time, keep to detailing only the last ten years of employment on your resume. For any work that is relevant to the job that you are applying for, have a section further down on your resume that is titled *'other employment'* and list it there. You don't need to go into too much detail in this section about the job and what you did, as long as whoever reads it can identify that it was more than ten years ago. You still want to make the company aware that you had that position, because it is relevant.

Your cover letter should also be tailored for each different position and company. If the application that you are sending off is from an advertisement for the job, then make sure you address in your cover letter, everything that is stated in the advertisement. If you're sending off an application through the hidden market, then include the experience that you possess that the company is looking for, which you have discovered during your research.

130

As I briefly mentioned above, while you're completing these things to obtain that dream job, always keep that positive mind frame. Like attracts like in today's world and potential employers can pick up on whether you really want the position and whether you believe in yourself. By giving off the energy that you believe in yourself, you give the employer the confidence to believe in you and this leads to showing them that you're the perfect fit for the job during your interview.

Never give up! Keep striving to accomplish what you set out to achieve and if you feel that you are unable to tackle the hurdle on your own, ask for help. There are many private recruitment agencies and employment professionals who can give you that needed guidance and support.

MANIFESTING A NEW LIFE

Compiled by **PATRICIA LEBLANC**

Short Manifesting Story #3

I had a Dream

By Farahana Surya Kassam

I had a dream. It was to bring love and light back into my life at a time when I was surrounded by a darkness that had consumed me for far too long. During my separation and divorce journey, regret, worry, guilt and disappointment were shackles that paralyzed me. The fear of the unknown of my future made me frightfully insecure. But despite it, the one thing that I knew was, going backwards was not an option. This light had to shine, and nothing or no one was going to have the power to dim it - ever! Writing became my escape and tool for healing. I spoke to God about my intentions and the reason and motivation behind these intentions. They came from the heart and would inspire others too.

I recall always feeling so guilty about praying to God during my difficult times. I felt that people were suffering more than I was. People were facing critical illness, disease, poverty, hunger and so many other atrocities in their lives. How could I possibly complain? During the marriage, we were financially blessed, we lived in a beautiful 5 bedroom home, drove fancy cars, we were blessed with a beautiful healthy son, I mean really, what more did I need? Why was there still a void deep down? I knew better though. Material wealth never did, never could and never would buy me the love I craved for so long.

What I finally understood was that I had been looking for love in all the wrong places and that realization began an internal shift. The barriers of communication that had existed for so long by that wall of fear had disabled my ability to listen to God and what He wants us all to know. Somehow, the darkest time of my life shone a light of awakening and everything began making sense. The shift opened up doors of communication that started giving me answers to all the questions I had been asking for years. God was communicating as He always had been doing, but finally I was learning to listen. I now know that signs, feelings, intuitions, sixth senses, gut feelings, "right place at the right time", "small world", "...but it all worked out at the end" encounters are all Him and as I follow His queues I am continuously led on my path of purpose.

God knows exactly how to communicate to each and every one of us, in a language that is loving, simple and easy to follow. All we need to learn to do is listen, follow the signs, and allow Him to guide us. Once we learn how to release our fears, and embrace every person and situation without judgment, we begin to receive and feel His love in ways we never imagined possible. That is when you start to co-create a life that is destined for you. Be love, be light, and stay in faith.

Angela Ong

As a Product Designer and Retail Merchandising Strategist, Angela helps her clients bring their ideas to life. She provides insight into the marketplace for start-up and growth stage retail business owners through strategic focus on trends, understanding their ideal target consumer, competitor, price, manufacture and product design solutions. For over thirteen years, she has honed her skill in commercial design, print and branding salable products for major global retailers. With her sharpened design and implementation skills, she offers her clients the expertise on how to craft the most inspired product that will incite them to sell.

To learn more about Angela, please visit:
http://www.angelaong.com

Looking to launch a product idea? You can also subscribe to her at:
http://www.designproductsthatsell.com

Chapter 16

Life Is A Creative Journey - Here Is Mine.

By Angela Ong

There is a painting that hangs on my wall that greets me every morning, noon and night: a mantra, an affirmation, and an inspiration that tells me everyday to "Do what you love. Love what you do".

As far back as I can remember, being creative meant everything that allowed me to scribble, write or draw on any available surface, be it an object, a wall, a doll, or a piece of scrap paper. Then there was the evolution of the performing artist in me, who had to move her body through gymnastics and balance beams, cartwheels and back flips, dancing and singing to any rhythm that kept my heart beat up and gave me a vehicle of expression.

This was my foundation for whom I have become today.
Over the years, I have been in transition mode with my career and the business that it has led me to. Being a creative person who always had the desire to connect my skill set to all the experiences I've accumulated over the years in my professional career and trainings. I learned at an early age that

it was my intuition that had me follow this journey. The road was not easy and there was no clear path for how my desired business would take shape, let alone manifest itself into what it has become today.

Had I stayed in the corporate world of apparel and product design, it would have taken me on an upward path professionally. Yet before I decided to venture into this new realm of entrepreneurship, the questions I faced spoke along the lines of:

"If I left, how would I survive?"
"Can I do this?"
"Am I nuts" and "What will become of me?"

Fear is a powerful parasite that will rule your thoughts should you allow it in. I decided that fear was a parasite that I had to learn to overcome. I could have stayed the course that my studies as an award winning design graduate took me, but in my heart, my soul and mostly in my head, I knew the path of the corporate life was not enough for me to do the meaningful work that I most desired.

Prior to this, I found myself making decisions based on the shoulds and shouldn'ts. It started at an early age, as all things do. Whether it was the result of my parents, teachers and society's teaching, this was what I learned, and how I created my own book of laws.

MANIFESTING A NEW LIFE

My traditional and cultural heritage carried with it a similar effect, as a first generation Canadian woman. I grew up in a family of self-made entrepreneurial immigrants. In 1979 my parents fled the war in Vietnam and survived the refugee camps. Arriving in Canada and later becoming Canadian Citizens, they built their business and a life for me and my brothers. Knowing what I know now, this was no easy feat, and I thank them not only for my life, but instilling in me that all is possible if we take the chance. No words can fully express my gratitude for the sacrifices they have had to overcome building something from nothing. Life for my parents was not easy, and perhaps that is why I have spent half of my adult life building a mountain of self-esteem for myself and my desires. I witnessed their pain, and at times their pain was transferred to me. The reality of it often left me spent and misguided. However, it is due to their courage and bravery that I am able to live in a free country, express my individuality and have the choice to move freely without fear. And that has been my constant self-guidance.

There have been many recounts where I experienced an invitation into the creative world. One was as early as grade school, where I had submitted a logo drawing into a competition that to this day, is still being used on the graduating class t-shirts. Later, I received notice that I was accepted into the Ryerson University of Fashion Design program in Toronto. I had been accepted into a creative world, one I loved, and one that would quantify me if I applied myself fully. Being surrounded by like minded talented students, I found myself not only excelling in my craft, but feeling humbled in an environment that was inspiring, collaborative and sharing interests with like minded peers. It is the competitive yet constructive environment that has helped me to continue excelling today.

It gave me a place to speak from. It put my pen to work on all surfaces again and to manifest a feeling and not just the aesthetic. Life no longer feels like a tightrope walk. I gracefully balance on the beam through connecting and facilitating others to realize their dream. I encourage my clients to exercise their creativity while I walk alongside them. I provide them with the tools to create their vision, get out of their head, and connect to what is really important to make their business thrive. I share my story to test their limits, rise above their preconceived notions of failure, and support and encourage them to simply go for it. Because after all, the methodology to designing a successful product is meant to help others while telling a great story. This is what I refer to as going beyond first impressions. I help my clients realize the potential in their brand, peel back the layers and get to the core of their idea and its essence. Together we bring it to market and plan for it to flourish.

MANIFESTING A NEW LIFE

As I continue to go through my creative journey, I am always seeking to manifest a better me. By doing this, I hope to encourage others to seek out the same so they can do what they love, and most importantly, love what they do.

Compiled by **PATRICIA LEBLANC**

Maryetta Jones

Entrepreneur-Student of Life, Woman Warrior.
Owner/Operator of Stonehouse Girl.
I was looking for the leverage to transition into something that was possible to commit to at this stage of my life. Following my dreams for a life lived with passion and freedom. I still want to create, I still want to work, and most of all I want to share with you, what this has given to me!

I am a dedicated hard working woman who draws from a deep well of experiences, and my quest is to help **build and transform** and brighten the world of all who may want to know her. Courage, my loves.

To learn more about Maryetta, please visit:
www.stonehousegirl.ca

You can also send her an email: maryetta@sympatico.ca

Chapter 17

Warrior Woman - Get in, Get Down, Get Dirty.

By Maryetta Jones

The effect you have on others is the most valuable currency there is. The flip side to this pancake is, if you accept the expectations of others, especially the negative ones, then you will never change the outcome.

I learned this at a very young age. You see I came from a large family, middle child, older siblings teaching me and younger siblings to teach. I was domesticated by parental and societal values that made very little sense to me, and at age fifteen, I declared war. I was coined a rebel, but I felt more like a Woman Warrior, so I ran headfirst into the unknown. My dreams were very alive and strong. I knew that's what was needed to be a great warrior who defends their life, their happiness and their freedom.

Our normal human tendency is to enjoy life, to play, to explore, to be happy, and to love; so what the hell happened to the adult life? I have fallen many times, but I stood back up and kept going through each and every shit-storm that came my way. Even when exhaustion set in and took up space I was never afraid to play. Tired yes, afraid no. Courage is my ally. Always right by my side, holding me up and moving me through the slippery slope of life's trenches.

Somewhere along this tricky terrain called adolescence, I knew intuitively that the world is a table full of bounty in which to feast. It is here for us to savour, explore, experience, learn, love, endure the pain and pleasure of the whole damn adventure. I had been raised feral. It was part of my genetic makeup, so finding my path and direction in life was completely natural to me, yet caused pain and anguish to those who did not share my dream.

Somehow, during this transition, I became an optimist: someone who recognized that taking a step backward after taking a step forward is not a disaster, it's more like a CHA-CHA.

All I had to do was ask myself this one question:
"Who do I un-become to become the person I want to be?"

My answer to self was,
"If it feels shitty, do less of it. If it feels good, do more of it. When you step outside your comfort zone, it expands you. Fuck fear, be courageous and make your own book of law."
Pretty profound for a fifteen year old girl, but hey, there you have it.

MANIFESTING A NEW LIFE

I lived most of my adult life in Toronto. As a child, I loved Sunday drives with my parents, and later, when I bought my first car, I would jump in it every chance I got and headed for the countryside.

I intuitively had an emotional connection to the open space, the winding country roads and the limitless sky. However it was my curiosity for the lovely old stone homes that sat back on the landscape at the end of a long driveway, which held my attention the most. They seemed so old, yet sturdy and strong, reminding me of renderings from childhood fairy tale books. Who lived in them? What did these people do? A minefield of imagination stirred within me.

After graduating from art college, I decided to take my first European Hejira journey, a pre-requisite for any young budding artist. My first adventure was England and OMG what an eye opener for this young Canadian girl. The little stone houses that speckled the Canadian countryside morphed into manors, mansions, cathedrals and castles. I fell in love all over again. The difference this time was that I was able to get inside them and the spell was cast, thanks to the National Trust Foundation.

A few years later I travelled to Italy. With the great unknown ahead of me once more, I accepted the invitation from inspiration to live in an old restored Tuscan farmhouse just south of the medieval fortress town of Montalcino, for the summer. This house seemed more proportional to our Canadian stone houses, but it was the view of the vineyards, the river running through the property, the people, their families, their love and connection to the land and what it produced, and those Tuscan sunsets that gave them such joy.

Many days Levio, our neighbouring farmer, would bring us fresh homemade bread, prosciutto he had smoked himself, (yup, he had to shoot that damn wild boar that was stomping on his award winning Brunello grapes), a basket of fresh peaches that were companion planted in his Brunello vineyard, and a bottle or two of the best Brunello di Montalcino wine I've ever tasted.

My most memorable moments stay with me and form my life story. Their stories became mine. These stories opened my eyes, my heart and soul. It was the impetus of this experience that determined the momentum for this woman warrior's fascinating journey. My life.

I adore stone houses, especially if a river runs through the property. For me, the river represents a constant movement of life, the stone structure is a solid framework and foundation, and most importantly this house has a history, and as we all know, a history gives us our stories.

MANIFESTING A NEW LIFE

I have lived in a few stone houses, let's call them a test run, but this STONEHOUSE girl is the cumulative seed that was planted long ago. It's both a retreat and a wellspring of inspiration that provides me continued growth and creativity. I have always enjoyed the process of building things and the need to work with my hands. For me there is a duty and a dedication that comes with it. Collaboration and inspiration walk hand in hand. This simple action has allowed me to transition and legitimise my enthusiasm, joy and balance in my day-to-day life. I call it my "Warrior Woman Happiness Project".

Coming from a busy city life, with an entrepreneurial background, I have had the opportunity to pursue many ventures. Be it in survival mode or thrival mode, I take action like a warrior anyway.

I was a Principal Partner in the graphic design firm Martin/Maryetta for sixteen years. During this chapter of my life, I also taught first year merchandising students basic design principals and colour theory at Seneca College in Toronto.

My love of brand building was the inspiration for my next venture Wallflower: a woman's boutique that included a branded line of signature products. The product range included apothecary, paper products, jewellery, clothing, linens and home décor, in a nutshell, much of what I love.

One of the highlights was to promote young talented Canadian designers, who too were warriors heading out into the unknown. This was my tribe. They were talented and curious, but they needed someone to collaborate with them. I saw this, while corporate leaders didn't, and I can tell you right now that many of those young designers have achieved great victories in their career. We believed as a tribe that there was enough bounty for all, the sky was limitless and we kicked ass - we fought for our freedom and we won.

The retail space was as imaginative in its presentation as it was exquisite in details. I understood the importance of distinctiveness, consistency and the quality of delivery. I liked to think of it as my guaranteed "must come again" experience. I employed these same creative and customer service skills at Rosetta, my award-winning restaurant that enjoyed much success and proved to be a destination for guests far beyond the immediate community. In addition to providing the most imaginative and rewarding dining experience, I fulfilled my love of cooking, plating food with feeling as well as an esthetic. Thank you once again Italy.

Enjoying travel, music, art and design, friendship and conversation, (all who know me will corroborate), I was looking for the leverage to transition into something that was possible to commit to at this stage of my life. I confess, all of my ideas have not been great, but I took action anyway. What inspiration teaches us, is this: if she knocks on your door, invite her in. Your dreams are very much alive and strong during this collaboration and this is where the Big Magic begins again, each and every time. The action alone is what makes me happy, even if in the end it was not a total success, taking the action is being alive. There really is no such thing as failure; it's just a thing that is trying to move you in another direction. Remember that you get as much from your losses as you do from your victories. Failure is a bruise, not a tattoo.

The great Sophia Loren said it best, "Our past mistakes are the dues we pay for having a full life". I absolutely agree, Sophia.

There will always be a challenge to work toward. Take the risk and I guarantee it will always lead to something. Trust your soul's compass and follow it. Be the great warrior who defends their life, their happiness and their freedom and remind yourself that your life is way bigger than any one experience.

Sometimes we forget the simple solutions, because it's not good business. How about this: instead of re-designing the air conditioner because it's ugly may I suggest opening a window.

What I know for sure: "Time is strange. We are all particles of change between the forceps and the stone therefore everyone and everything becomes more precious." A valuable currency indeed!

MANIFESTING A NEW LIFE

Rachel Vdolek

Rachel Vdolek is a multi-passionate entrepreneur who loves to teach others how to boost their confidence and self-esteem so they can create amazing lives that are better than their dreams. She also loves to cook, ski, hike and travel around her native Pacific Northwest.

You can find her at facebook.com/rachelvdolek or Instagram instagram.com/glowyourbusiness and see her travels at instagram.com/huckleberries.and.rain

Chapter 18

How I Manifested my Perfect cat... And an Extra one too

By Rachel Vdolek

I love cats. I've always had a cat for most of my life. But when I moved from my apartment to a house, I didn't have a cat. My previous cat, George, had passed away a few months before and I was missing him terribly.

My fiancé, however, is not a cat person. He is not a pet person at all. So when I asked if we could get a cat for our new home, he said: "not now".

Suffice it to say, I wasn't very happy.

So I manifested a cat instead!

The first time I tried it, it went exactly as I had asked for, but not as I had planned. When I was thinking of a cat, I was thinking of a super snuggly, friendly, loving cat who would be my best furry friend. What I had asked for was 3 cats to be hanging out around our new house.

And I got 3 cats that liked to hang out around our new house, but all 3 would run away as soon as they saw us.

Not really what I had wanted.

After about 6 months of getting frustrated, because none of the cats wanted anything to do with me, I decided to get more specific.

I asked for a cat that was friendly and would let me pet it.

A few days later, my fiancé came home with kitty treats he bought at the store. I tried feeding them to one of the cats, but I had to throw them a few feet away from me in order to get her to eat them. Oh did she love them. She would gobble them up, but if I got too close, she would still run away.

After a few weeks of daily treats, my fiancé came home with a bag of kitty food. (Mind you, I never asked him to get some. He just went and got it himself!) I started leaving bowls of food out for her when I saw her hanging out in the garden. She was still very apprehensive about me getting close, but eventually she let me pet her.

We became fast friends after that. She began to look forward to the petting and hanging out together on the deck more than the food. I named her Ellie after my great aunt. I had hoped for an orange cat, because they are my favorite, but she was all colors of the kitty rainbow. She had orange, brown and tan with black stripes and spots.

Since it was summer, I was spending a lot of time with her on the deck. I was enjoying petting her and feeding her, but what I really wanted was a lap cat. I always loved having a cat sit on my lap and purr while I knit or watch TV, but she was an outdoor semi-feral cat. I didn't think she would even consider being a lap cat.

But I asked anyways.

The next day, I was sitting in my chair on the deck and all of a sudden, she jumped into my lap! She purred and purred and dug her claws into my leg as a sign of affection before curling up and snoozing in my lap.

I was one happy woman.

Until the summer came to an end. It started to get rainy and stormy out, as fall usually is in the Pacific Northwest. I was worried that she wouldn't come back and I would lose my furry friend.

So I asked that she become an indoor cat who could use a litter box with no problems.

Next thing I know, my fiancé is letting her inside the house. This is the same man that said he did not want a cat. He had grown fond of her and how sweet she was. Plus she would kick the butt of any dog or other animal that came through our yard, so he loved that she was also a tough kitty.

It turns out she knew exactly how to use a litter box and so she quickly got comfortable snoozing on our couch.

She has now become my little baby. Every morning she cries for me to come sit with her on the couch while I drink my tea and every evening she curls up in my lap for snuggles while we watch TV before bed. She has even taken to loving and repeatedly asking for chin and belly scratches!

Did I mention that I accidentally manifested a second cat? I was so happy about the first one that I asked for another cat, but I forgot to be specific.

He started coming around about mid-summer, after Ellie and I had become friends, but Ellie wasn't happy. He was a tiny little black kitty and he loved Ellie. But Ellie didn't want anything to do with him.

MANIFESTING A NEW LIFE

We named him Loki, because he was such a troublemaker. He would climb all over our house and bang his head against the door when he wanted food. He would disappear for a few days then come back. He grew very rapidly into one of the biggest cats I'd ever seen.

He was definitely someone's cat, because he was always very well fed, so we kept him outdoors. We still see him sporadically, especially early in the mornings when he still bangs his head against the door, saying, "Feed me!" He won't let us pet him, unless his head is buried in his food bowl.

Tip for manifesting: Get super clear on what you want, otherwise you may end up with something that is close, but not exactly right.

Mariana Calleja

Mariana Calleja is a doctor, pain management specialist and holistic health advocate helping people heal their chronic pain and emotional pain, allowing them to move forward towards a better quality of life. As a world traveller, writer, thinker, and former sexual pain sufferer, Mariana is up for deep truthful talks, breaking taboos, traveling the world, and writing openly about it all.

Social media links:

www.facebook.com/marianacallejaross

www.instagram.com/doctor.mariana

Website:

www.marianacalleja.com

Chapter 19

How to Manifest a New You Through Travel

By Mariana Calleja

It all starts with travel.

Travel has been my guiding passion, my true north towards what feels right and makes the most sense in my life. I still remember my first flight, age seven, crossing the Caribbean Sea to San Andres Island, far from the coast between Nicaragua and Colombia. It's still a potent, evocative memory of sensations and images... and the feeling of something momentous beginning in my life.

I used to have a recurring dream for many years where the aircraft I was on would drive on the highways of my small city - never lifting off the ground. After a few trips and endless "highway aircraft" dreams, I decided at age 13 that I wanted to go as far away as I could, the furthest into the unknown that I could envisage and engineer for myself - and I fixated on Barcelona as the other side of the world. I wrote its name on my heart, and that longing stayed with me.

We all have dreams. How many of them turn into reality? None of them, unless we decide to *make* them reality.

January 22nd, 2010

I'm sleepy. It's been a long night. I fight to keep my eyes open as I gaze at the crisp morning outside the window. The sky is shades of pink, orange and light blue. The sun isn't out yet, but morning light is pouring softly into the world. Far in the distance I can see the most stunning snow-capped mountains I've ever seen in my life: my first sight of the Pyrenees.

However bitterly cold it is out there, I'm warm and comfy in my window seat. The flight attendant offers tea for breakfast as she walks through the aisle. With a huge smile creasing my tired face, I pinch myself: "Mariana, my dear, we're almost there... Barcelona!"

***

Thirteen years had passed since I decided I had to try to get to Barcelona. Thirteen years of finding a way to make my dream about this place turn into something tangible - and today I'm sitting on a flight, about to land in the place of my heart's calling. And my happiness is laced with doubt.

MANIFESTING A NEW LIFE

Would I like it?
What if I *don't*?
What if it's a thirteen-year flight of fantasy that's about to be exposed as a lie?

This was the first time I allowed myself to ask these questions. I was so convinced of the need to try that there was no room for doubt or fear in me. But that was easy when I wasn't actually here, facing the moment of truth.

I've manifested Barcelona for myself - and I was about to find out if it was the right decision.

And that's travel, every time. You leap, you hope, you find out in person. That's the deal you make with the world - and I've never regretted making it.

So, why travel?

Why has travel been so important, so close to my heart more than anything else?

Maybe it's the challenge. Because, wow, travel pushes you to all your limits. As much as it's a calling, it's almost a supreme act of will. I just followed it as hard as I could, throwing everything I've got into the mix and hoping it's enough to get me there in one piece. The result is a constantly evolving level of adventure where I'm pressed up against the limits of what my mind and body can accomplish - constantly growing, constantly being pushed to grow.

That never gets easier. I don't expect it ever will - and I hope not, because that's the rush of it.

Travel manifests a sense of independence like nothing else I've found. It was travel that allowed me to become the grownup I dreamed of, far beyond from my formal education at home. It was travel that opened me up to new horizons, dreams, thoughts, ideas, possibilities, challenges, actions, connections, people, opportunities and ways of expressing myself, in my own language and in others I eagerly learned.

Travel above all, opened me up to become my best self ever. It showed me who I could grow into - and why I'd want to.

It's been a constant evolution and clarification of self that has taught me to serve others in greater and more effective ways, whether it's my family, my partner, my patients, my readers, my friends, my colleagues, my neighbours and beyond.

A Chronology Of Change

If I have to write a chain of fortunate events that unlocked my inner self through travel, it would look something like this:

MANIFESTING A NEW LIFE

An early obsession with world geography and aircraft (don't ask me where *that* came from).

Getting a major inner call from Barcelona at age 14.

Arriving in Barcelona at age 27.

My first experience of living, working and studying abroad.

Learning a new culture, new languages, new lifestyles and different ways of thinking.

Redefining home and laying down new roots.

Mariana 1.0 becomes v2.0 - more confident, worldly, able to deal with uncertainty and to think on her feet.

New experiences (largely environmental) rewiring my sense of self.

Realising I unlocked a new reality for myself - and realising that's what dreams are *for*.

Being in awe became my new normal.

Deciding it's time to create Mariana v3.0 - and starting the whole process over again, by thinking "What's my *next*

Barcelona? What are my *new* horizons? What's the *next* journey I need to take, in a literal and metaphorical sense?

From past experience, knowing it won't happen unless I really go for it.
I really go for it.
A new cycle of growth begins.

February 12th, 2017

I'm sitting in my lovely terrace full of light, fresh air and green plants at my current new home in Costa Rica - my next destination after seven years abroad and 18 months of nomadic travel and business-building mode.

En route to my next journey, I've come full circle. I'm here to recharge and reflect on who I am now and what I want next. I know it is time to lay down new roots elsewhere - and this is the right place to decide where those roots lay. My inner GPS led me here, and it's the right place to decide. I trusted it, as I always do, and yet again, it guided me true.

But there's another circle at work here.

I manifest travel for myself - and travel manifests *me*.

MANIFESTING A NEW LIFE

Round and round we go. Everything changes. The center cannot hold, and has no wish to do so either. Everything is movement and progress and evolution - and the scenery is terrific too.

It's an exciting life.

You never know who you'll be at the end of it.

HOW TO MANIFEST A NEW YOU THROUGH TRAVEL

1. You can choose to go anywhere. Seriously. Don't kid yourself with worries about money, timing, commitments. They might be obstacles, but there's always a way round them, if you're prepared to work hard and smart enough and not get there as fast as other people. And if you really, really *care*, you'll do all these things. Fact.
2. Anyone who says it's "just a dream", including that voice deep inside, is correct in once sense, and dead wrong in another. Your heart knows which of these *really* matters.
3. Commit. Forget practicalities - they'll come later. Commit **now**.
4. Freak out. (Required! Yes, it can feel scary and confusing and also feel like something you can't not do - all at the same time. This is not a sign you're going crazy. This is an indication that you're going *sane*.)

5. Change the world. Not all of it. Just your corner of it. Get to work, make it happen, go to your dream place and do that dream thing, until you can edit out the word "dream" because it's your new normal. If it takes 13 years? Whatever! That's what it takes.
6. Stop in the street one day and realise you're now a completely different person.
7. Freak out again. See: (4).
8. Realise you completely rebuilt yourself from the ground up - by changing the ground first. How about that?
9. Enjoy this for a while. You've earned it.
10. Go back to (1).

MANIFESTING A NEW LIFE

Erica Stepteau

Erica Stepteau is an Empowerment & Tenacity Coach who empowers women to be tenacious on their journey by pushing beyond thoughts of scarcity, past failures, potential obstacles, and lack of resources. We all have infinite power within to claim our birthright of inheritance. Most of the time it's our emotional baggage and gremlins (inner chatter) preventing us from being "unstoppable". Tenacity is a learned trait and *Unstoppable Tenacity* provides the blueprint on how to create the life you have always dreamed of. Erica is the #1 Best Selling Author of *Unstoppable Tenacity*, available on Amazon and Barnes and Noble websites.

You can connect with Erica
On Facebook: https://www.facebook.com/unstoppabletenacity
On Instagram: Erica_stepteau
On Linkedin: https://www.linkedin.com/in/erica-stepteau-mph-chc-3651aa44/

Chapter 20

Own your Money Story to Become a Money Magnet

By Erica Stepteau

During my childhood, my family would gather at my grandparents' home to bring in the New Year. This particular year was no different than other years; there was a ton of food in the kitchen including my grandfather's delicious ribs with his amazing homemade barbeque sauce. My uncles were in the backyard firing their guns, and a group of other family members were gambling on my grandparents' slot machine in their living room and playing Pokeno at the dining room table.

Our family's favorite gambling game was Pokeno: a hybrid of poker and bingo played with a 52-card deck. Each player is given a Pokeno board, similar to a bingo card consisting of 25 squares (Five rows each with five squares). A dealer gradually uncovers and announces each card of the deck, with players attempting to complete a row of five cards using counters to cover each card on the board as it is announced. My family would take it to the next level and have money pots for following additional accomplishments: 4 corners, Center, 4 of a kind, and of course Pokeno (5 across, down, or diagonally).

Typically, they would use coins to put in the "pot"; each game could cost a quarter, dime, or even a penny for each Pokeno board you have with each game. Everything depended on what the dealer declared before the round started. Some family members would have as many as 5 boards at a time.

This was a symbolic year for me. I was finally old enough to gamble with the family (approximately 14 years old). The feeling was surreal. I had watched from the sidelines for years as everyone played and left the table with buckets of money. I would dream about what I would buy with the money. One of my dreams was to buy a pair of Michael Jordan tennis shoes since I was playing basketball at the time. I would imagine getting a red, black, and white pair and how those shoes would give me the speed and hops I needed to effectively play on my team. I felt giddy and super excited to await my turn for a chance to make my dream come true. After a few people dropped out of the game, I was asked if I wanted to join. I anxiously said "Yes!" Then I straightened up my voice to act cool and calm, because in my head I was thinking, adults don't get this excited to play Pokeno. I had to make sure I was blending in and not being too anxious.

When I sat in the hot seat, instantly an overwhelming feeling hit me. I was thinking to myself *wow, this time I am hanging out with the 'big dawgs'*. I felt powerful and over the moon. My heart was racing and my knees were shaking. I was emulating

169

everything I had witnessed through the years. If you were a fly on the wall you would see me grinning ear to ear with beads of sweat on my top lip and forehead as I began to get into the game. We were playing for a while (approximately 30 minutes or so) and actually having fun. Everyone was laughing and making fun of each other on their losses and celebrating their wins. You could probably hear all the laughter and chatter several houses away. My younger cousins and sister were running around playing with one another on the first floor of the home and in the basement. The aroma of grandpa's sauce filled the home along with the other typical foods of greens, mac & cheese, yams, and dessert.

We continued to play Pokeno as the money pots for 4 corners and 4 of a kind built up. The game ends when someone gets Pokeno (5 across, down, or diagonally). If no one wins the other pots, then it just rolls over to the next game. We were playing for quarters and it had to be a few hours at this point, because the 4-corner pot was overflowing; it had to be at least $50-60 worth of quarters in the pot. I just knew that amount could cover my Jordan's. As we continued to play, the concentration increased among the group. The room began to silence more as we intensely awaited the cards to be called out by the dealer.

I was one card away and just waited silently for my King of hearts to be called. About 3 seconds later, my card was called and I hesitated, because I wanted to make sure I was calling out the right win before shouting "4 corners!" out loud. When I spoke up the next card was being called at the same time, and I said, "Wait...hey, I got 4 corners"! A family member said to me with no thought or remorse, "well you missed your chance, you shouldn't be so slow. You lost your chance". I was crushed and couldn't believe that a family member twice my age would even be so aggressive with me over that pot of money. My Jordan dream was crushed right at that moment. From this moment on, this story shaped how I ran my personal finances and how I felt about money.

After the incident with my family, I vowed to never gamble again. Isn't it funny when we declare such a bold statement and find ourselves still falling in the trap? My whole life I have gambled with money, but in a very different way than expected. With the help of a coach I discovered my money story and realized I was acting out my worst fear.

Gambling. Merriam-Webster defines it as a game of chance; to bet on an uncertain outcome; to stake something on a contingency: take a chance.

When I approached the table to join my family for my first round of gambling, I felt empowered, on cloud 9, and excited about what money could provide me: my Jordan's. When the dream was taken from me, I began to feel powerless, devalued, and very frustrated about money. These same traits have carried on in my adult life. I basically "gambled" my finances from one check to another, because it gave me a rush and a huge thrill and helped me escape my frustrations with money. I wasn't in a casino gambling my money, but I had a gambler's mindset". Most of my adult life I frowned upon budgets, or any organization with money. In addition, every time I would have a financial setback it would feel just like that moment at the table: the feelings of lack of power, overwhelm, and frustration.

To attract a steady money-flow in your life, you must learn how to view money not as a thing merely, but as an expression of energy- ultimately, as an expression of your own energy. As I invested the time and energy to explore my feelings and disbeliefs, I realized this story connected heavily to my underlying root issue blocking abundance in my life. I began to do inner work and created reframes for the disbeliefs to clear those blocks. Within 90 days of this inner work, I received $26,939.64 in cash and gifted services!

Your story may not be the same as mine, but take some time right now and think about your money story. Do you live paycheck to paycheck or client to client and wonder how bills will get paid at times? Do you dread looking at your budget or planning finances? Have you found yourself sabotaging yourself through thoughtless spending habits? Are you tired of hustling for money? If you have been struggling with consistent overflow of abundance in your life and suffering from feast and famine syndrome, there is an underlying root reason why you do what you do. There is a reason for everything. It's your job to uncover the possible culprit, which keeps you in this cycle. I will show you how:

- What was your earliest memory about money?
- Did your family experience a defining moment around money? A defining moment shapes our beliefs – we take away a meaning from that experience.

- Now write one paragraph..." My current relationship with money is...." How is that story still affecting your current money mindset?
- Start a **'Money Journal'** to explore your relationship with money, added value, and outgoing expenses. Download *Unstoppable Tenacity* money journal here: www.unstoppabletenacity.com
- Write about what's working, what feels good, and when and where do you feel frustrated and powerless or just not right.

MANIFESTING A NEW LIFE

Compiled by **PATRICIA LEBLANC**

Short Manifesting Story #4

Born to Believe That I Can Receive

By Lisa E. Harris Gore, MBA

What if you were born to believe that you got everything you EVER wanted? What if you could see it, feel it, imagine already having it and were blessed enough to have it appear in front of you in the least expected ways? You know, delivered by a truck, by car, special delivery, FedEx, a friend, a relative, a classmate, a co-worker, a mentor, a teacher, a spouse or even a stranger?

It would be amazing, wouldn't it? Well, here's a little story about my awakening to the possibilities of "getting" whatever it was I could imagine.

I was raised in a blue collar working family. Hard work was how you got "things". Hard work was how you "earned" a better life and if you didn't work hard, you would be poor, on the streets and eating out of a garbage can. Almost every day, I would hear that we didn't have enough money. It's what my parents would argue over.

MANIFESTING A NEW LIFE

I never asked for much as a child, because I believed that it wasn't worth the pain of seeing my parents struggle for more money just so I could have something. Most of the toys I had as a baby, toddler or young child were given to me, and sometimes they weren't even a toy at all. You know those kinds of toys, the cardboard box, the jar of coins that a baby probably shouldn't be playing with... I do remember a big ball that I enjoyed when toddling around and a few stuffed animals... but all the "cool" stuff that I wanted as I got older had to wait until it was my turn to work HARD... and so I did. At the age of 12, I started my first job and decided that I would work to get the things I wanted.

I remember being a bit of a daydreamer. What I was doing was imagining things that I desired to be different in my life. When I saw something in my mind that would make my life better, I consciously DECIDED that it would be mine and it literally became my reality. At that time, I didn't know what manifestation was. All I knew was suddenly it started working. I wanted a piano and one day I came home to a beautiful piano that I randomly decided I wanted, but never asked for. I wanted to own my first car and a friend unexpectedly purchased one for me. I would play around to see if it was just coincidental and quickly discovered not only did good things start to happen, but so did the things that I worried about. If an image of a deer came to my mind while driving, moments later a deer would cross in front of my vehicle.

In college I had been practicing a lot of meditation and discovered that the more "in-tune" I became the more accurate I could be. I hadn't done much research on what was happening, but could confidently say, "Whatever it is that I truly desire, can come to be real." What I noticed was that if I had heightened awareness, then it was nearly 100% accurate.

My mother currently says to my children, "Your mother NEVER had even a fraction of what you all have when she was your age." I find this statement a reminder of how to be mindful of what I teach my kids about money, abundance and manifestation. Today I live in the home I dreamed of living in as a child. I have the 4 kids I imagined having 20 years ago, the husband that fits my perfect husband list that I described 26 years ago, the cars, the "stuff", the friends, the businesses, the... everything I ever "wished for."

How did I go from a place of a lacking mentality to a life of abundance? How did I manage to transition the feeling of not having enough to one day awakening to having everything I could ever want? I believed, I often took action, I wraped that with the feeling of it already being real and I opened myself up to receive. I was born to believe that I can receive good things in all the days of my life. Therefore... I do, and so can YOU.

MANIFESTING A NEW LIFE

Jennifer Low

Jennifer has always loved to write and is now pursuing this more actively as a writer, compiler, editor, and ghostwriter. She is an international best-selling author and has been published several times.

Jennifer is committed to respectful empowerment and is dedicated to adding polish to people who are seeking that higher standard. She does this in the writing world, as well as through coaching and mentoring. Jennifer is helping people realize their true potential, reach their goals and achieve true success. She is also an excellent mother and a great investor.

You can contact her at:

http://anauthenticu.com/

https://www.facebook.com/anauthenticu/?fref=hovercard

https://www.linkedin.com/in/jennifer-low-812a2716

Chapter 21

Twenty Years in the Making

By Jennifer Low

The act of writing to be published is really about sharing your treasures with the world. It is about creating a visibility in your message, letting people know you are there, you exist, and to share your knowledge and wisdom.

My writing "career" really started when I was a young pre-teen. At 9 years old, I left Canada and moved to Europe, away from my extended family and friends. We didn't have the internet at the time. So the only way for me to communicate was through letters. When you send a letter to someone, and it gets opened in anticipation and read, as the writer you have the full attention of that reader, wouldn't you say? It felt comforting and fulfilling for me to be "heard" because somehow that wasn't really encouraged among my immediate family.

I have always wanted to work from home. During the many years I was a stay-at-home mom, I always had this thought in the back of my mind of being able to make an income from home. Something that was just for me. I wanted to have some money come my way, but most of all I wanted to feel productive and valuable within my family as well as in the marketplace.

In 2008, this became a necessary reality! My husband left and now it was all on me! How was I going to do this? I wanted to still be at home with my kids and stay flexible to keep them as my priority, but now I had to seriously find a way to be making some cash from home. Having grown up trilingual, I figured translation could provide me with such an opportunity. I was to pursue my third University degree with this one.

Let's fast forward…
In December of 2014, I was casually asked over a coffee if I knew of anyone who would like to write and be published. What an odd question, I thought! How about meee?!!
Honestly, at first, I was quite shy about it. The person who had asked me this had already been published multiple times and I had absolutely no credibility in writing what so ever. Why would this person want to work with me? Then I waited stupidly in the background for her to approach me again about it. It never happened…

One day, I happen to fall upon a picture of this future book cover via social media. Woah! I had to act. This deserved a phone call and now!!

MANIFESTING A NEW LIFE

I called this lady up and asked in an excited and absolutely determined manner: "I know I belong behind that cover, what must I do to be part of this?" And so, my professional writing journey truly took off.

In January of 2015, I signed up to be part of *Manifesting a New Life*, book one. I was so incredibly excited about this project that every time I would meet someone with a great manifesting story I would ask if they would like to share it and connected them with the book compiler.

In the fall of that same year, the book was launched for the world to see and read, and I was published for the first time. Wow! What a sensation that was. What I was most excited about was the power this written word would have in the world, now and in the years ahead. My messages were getting released out of me and into the minds and the ideas of others. Powerful!

So in January of 2016, this same compiler approached me with my next challenge: create my own book of stories. What? Me? No! Not now! Not yet! I wasn't ready!! I had written one 1500 word chapter. How could I get this done? How could I think that big that quickly? Didn't I need to gradually build myself up?

Thing is, I was more ready than I ever thought I could be. I was challenged, I had a vision, I took action. And a year later, my own anthology book was released to the world. Oh, am I ever proud!

It's easy for me to say this now, of course.
The end result is always easily relished with glory. Yet, the journey to getting my book done was nothing short of hair ripping "impossible" at times! First I had to find the people, then have a conversation with them, then find out if it was something that interested them, then it was follow up and in some cases, it was follow up, follow up, and follow up again!
Twice I had set a due date for myself. Twice I had set myself a goal that I wasn't able to achieve. Twice I felt like this couldn't work and questioned myself on what I was doing and why. And twice I almost threw in the towel!

The most difficult part for me was to "sell" people on my idea. I knew so many entrepreneurs with a great story that I figured it would be easy to find authors. What I hadn't considered is that not everyone is as motivated to be published and may not love writing and value the written word as much as I do.

The first person I asked didn't say yes, but didn't say no either. Hmm… I left her on the fence. Next!
I remember the third call I placed. I was so nervous. Not only was I fed up of hearing "no", but I really wanted this man's story, because I found him to be truly embodying on the subject of choice. There was no better fit for my book than

him. He was my first yes! I was incredibly grateful. And now I was responsible to deliver, so I was truly committed to taking the next step and the next step after that. There was no turning back.

I believe it was blind faith and tenacity that kept this project going all the way through to the end.
I would find a bunch of people to ask, and lots of interest, but no sign ups. I was saddened that they couldn't see it for themselves and I was frustrated too. Frustrated that they couldn't pick a side and make a decision, and sometimes frustrated with my inability to effectively sell. At least that's what I told myself. Yet, this wasn't my decision to make. I was looking for people who were looking to ally with me! This is where I would breathe deeply and allow for the "outside forces" to help me out, to support me, and to bring forward the right people. I trusted. I simply had to!

I would then remind myself that quitting was not an option and I encouraged myself to find another door. I couldn't give up, because I had people who had already signed up and committed to my project, who were putting their trust in me to create a finished product. After all, I was the one who had sold them on my idea… I had to make sure I would see it through all the way. In reality, the role my co-authors played for me was that they were my silent accountability partners. I am grateful for it, as it gave me the strength I needed to carry on and it also made me grow a little more.

Every time I would hit a lull in sign ups, I would go look for the door that had a bright light shining around it and made sure to go open it. I trusted that all the right people would show up. I trusted I would manifest all the right people at my door and in the right time. And they did! I trusted that my guardian angels were looking out for me and that they always knew something I didn't.

At times, when I didn't feel like this project was advancing, I would remind myself that I was reaching out to the 20% of successful people I knew and that only the 1% was to be part of my book. Perspective is often my best remedy.

Manifesting is a process. This not only takes belief and action but also patience and faith. It is often a team sport: making anything happen often requires a team! One must not forget the power in masses.

With my book, *Peeking Behind The Scenes*, I have not only created my life moving forward, but I have also manifested my future by pre-paving it carefully.

And after 20 some odd years, I have also manifested my perfect working-from-home job: that of writer, editor, ghostwriter, and translator. I love what I do, I love putting polish to people, and their success fulfills me and makes me proud.

MANIFESTING A NEW LIFE

Patricia LeBlanc

Patricia LeBlanc is a Dream Maker. She empowers Spiritual Female Entrepreneurs to get out of their own way so that they can create the life and business that they desire. Patricia helps her clients get clear on what they want, release their money blocks and charge what they are truly worth.

Patricia is an Award winning Author, Compiler and Publisher, International Speaker and Trainer, Manifesting and Business Strategist as well as a Master Energy Healer and Teacher.

Let Patricia help you like she has helped thousands before you. Apply for your free consultation by visiting www.YourAbundanceCoach.com/Consultation

You can contact Patricia by Email: info@patricialeblanc.ca or info@manlpublishing.com

Chapter 22

It took 25 Years to Achieve my Childhood Dream

By Patricia LeBlanc

Recently, I got together with one of my best childhood friends. We had not seen one another in 17 years. During our conversation, she asked if I was working for myself or whether I still had a corporate job? I replied: "Yes I only work for myself and for my company". She reminisced how as a child I used to say that I would own my own business even though I didn't know the nature of what it would be. She also noted that I had realized my childhood dream.

This made me stop and think…

When we busy ourselves with manifesting, we usually want it NOW! It took me more than 25 years to manifest my dream business.

Growing up, I always knew that I wanted to be a businesswoman and help make the world a better place. I just didn't know what this would look like at the time. When I graduated from High School, I decided to go to College and get a degree in Small Business Management. This course was all about starting and running a business. It was a 2-year college course condensed in one year. It was very intensive.

I was all pumped to start my own business, but needed to figure out in what field.

After graduating from College, I decided to go to University, as I still had no idea what type of business I wanted to create. I did not like University and I only lasted a year and half.

During my University years I was introduced to network marketing. I joined what would end up being one of many network-marketing companies. I was so introverted and shy that I did nothing except buy some products and go to some of the meetings and personal development events. This was my introduction to personal development. It was the only part that I enjoyed in the business.

After University, I returned to the fast food restaurant I used to work at when I was 16. Soon after, I was promoted to supervisor and was responsible for opening and closing 4 restaurants in my area. After a few years, my boss asked me if I wanted to move up and become an assistant manager or a manager. If I was planning on staying with the company for years to come, I may as well advance while I studied business in school.

MANIFESTING A NEW LIFE

That made me think...

Then, one day, a manager position came up and I decided to apply. Everyone kept telling me I didn't stand a chance, as I was up against the two best contenders who were currently higher ranked than me. I knew deep down that something positive would come out of this. The day of my interview, I told the director of operations that if I was still a supervisor in 6 months then I would leave. I told him that I was willing to move to another city, as the company owned over 20 franchises in 2 provinces. I was even willing to move to Nova Scotia. He told me not to worry, and that he was keeping me in one of his stores. A month later, an Assistant Manager position came up in my area and it was basically mine.

Nine months later, I became a Manager and moved to Saint John, New Brunswick, to manage one of their stores. I figured once I was a manager for 2 years and had senior management experience behind me, I would start my own company.

I ended up signing up to 2 more networking marketing companies and experienced no success, but was blessed with more personal development. After spending several thousands of dollars, I came to realize that network marketing was not for me. Disappointed, I gave up any hope of ever having my own business.

Exactly 2 years after being promoted to Manager, I left that restaurant job to go work for a call center. This began my career of working in call centers.

In 2004, I was diagnosed with a major clinical depression and this was my wake up call. I no longer recognize who I was. I also realized that I was not living the life that I always dreamed of as a child.

From 2006 to 2008, I worked for myself as a massage therapist and it was a real struggle. I was just making ends meet and never knew where my next meal was going to come from or how I was going to pay my rent the following month.

In December 2008, I made a decision to go find a job as I was fed up of struggling financially. Within 2 days, I had found a small contract that would last a few months. I was again in the corporate world.

In 2012, I was in a car accident and almost died. I instinctively knew that the next time the Universe would throw me a curve ball I would not survive it. This was my wakeup call as I realized that I was heading in the wrong direction again and needed to do to something different.

I started studying and got certified in Law of Attraction, master life coaching, and abundance attraction. Many more certifications followed.

MANIFESTING A NEW LIFE

In 2015, I created what is now the International Best Selling Book Series called *Manifesting a New Life*. This is when I started releasing my visibility blocks as well as getting over my hatred of public speaking.

By the end of 2015, I was on burn out as I had been over exerting myself and had been working with the wrong clients. I fired 90-95% of my clients as they were draining me.
It was back to the drawing board. I had to become crystal clear on who I wanted to work with, and what results I could help them with.

2016 turned out to be my most successful year and my worst year so it was quite a rollercoaster. I learned so many life lessons, one of which was that I needed to start charging for my services.

2016 marked the first year that I was 100% self-employed and my business was supporting me at 100%. I did not need to go and get another job or contract work. I did not worry about how I was going to pay the bills. I was finally realizing my dream of being a self-supported entrepreneur.

In 2016, I finally got my dream business and in 2017 all of my childhood dreams are coming to fruition. I have a successful business with 2 divisions: a publishing company, as well as my coaching and healing business.

I am working with the most amazing clients, money is abundant, and I am surrounded by the most amazing people. Currently, I have a list of people waiting to work with me and I am attracting the most amazing opportunities. I am 100% abundant and aligned with my life mission, and I have never been happier.

I needed to have faith and believe that my dreams would happen. It took me between 25 and 30 years to make my childhood dreams come true. I never ever gave up and I am now building my own business empire. I have manifested my dream life and business.

I am now an International Manifesting and Business Strategist, Master Energy Healer and Teacher, International Speaker and Trainer, 16 Time International Best Selling Author, I have appeared on virtual summits with the likes of Dr. Joe Vitale and Marie Diamond from the Secret, and I have people coming to me to interview me. Money, ideas, great people and abundance keep flowing to me every day. I have interviewed some really amazing people on my podcast as well as on my upcoming manifesting and healing summit.

I was not always this successful, but I kept working towards my goals and dreams. I never ever gave up and let me tell you I came close, at least 100 times. I believed that I would create my dream life and business. I got out of my comfort zone.

MANIFESTING A NEW LIFE

Things really moved forward when I became aligned with myself and embraced myself fully.

If I could do it so can you. I had everything going against me and I still manifested my dream business.
Believe in yourself and anything is possible.

If you would like help in manifesting the life and business of your dreams, please do not hesitate to schedule your free consultation with me as it would be an honor to help you.

Happy Manifesting!

Conclusion

My hope with this book is that you realize just how powerful of a co-creator you are. My hope is that you realize that you can co-create anything that your heart desires and that there is enough abundance for everyone.

I want to encourage you to go back and read through this when you need to be inspired. If any of my co-authors' chapters, including my own, resonated with you, please reach out to them or to me to see how we can help you manifest a new life. We want to help you create the life and business that you want.

Always remember there is enough abundance for everyone. You are worthy of living a happy and abundant life. You have the power of manifesting anything that you truly want.

What small action step will you take today to achieve your goals and dreams? You can do it! I believe in you, but do you believe in YOU?

MANIFESTING A NEW LIFE

Various Ressources

Manifesting a New Life: Money, Love, Health and Everything in Between. Get your copy at www.ManifestingaNewLife.com

Manifesting a New Life: Your Magical Guide to Attracting the Life that you want. Get your copy at www.ManifestingaNewLife.com

Here are a several free resources to help you get to the next level.

The Spiritual Entrepreneur Show. You can listen right here: http://www.loalifecoaching.com/spiritual-entrepreneur-show and don't forget to download your free gift.

Manifesting + Healing for Spiritual Entrepreneur Facebook Group. You will receive support, various ressources, training, and tips on manifesting and energy healing. You will get support by Manifesting Expert and Master Energy Healer Patricia LeBlanc. You can join us here: https://www.facebook.com/groups/PatriciaLeBlanc/

MANIFESTING A NEW LIFE

On the last Sunday of the Month, I offer free long distance energy healing to everyone who sign up to receive it. You just need to sign up once and you will continue to receive the monthly healing as long as you remain on the list. Register for free here: http://www.loalifecoaching.com/free-monthly-healing

If you are ready to get out of your own way and start creating the life and business that you truly desire, please apply for your free consultation to see how I can serve you just like I did for thousands before you. Don't delay, apply today! www.talkwithpatricia.com

I am looking forward to help you to get to the next level. Always remember that there is enough abundance for everyone and success belongs to you.

Much Love and Gratitude,

Patricia xo

Do you dream of being published?

A book is one of the best way to increase your visibility, to increase your clientele, and to gain instant credibility.

If you want to turn your dream of publishing your own anthology book into reality, I will show you how to compile your own book, together, we can accomplish this cost free for you while you get paid to publish your own anthology book.

I can help you with your solo book publishing needs as well. Contact me about my various publishing packages.

If you want to turn your dream of publishing into reality contact me at info@manlpublishing.com

Talk to you soon,
Patricia LeBlanc

Manifesting + Healing
for Spiritual Entrepreneurs
with
Patricia LeBlanc
www.LoaLifeCoaching.com

Are you ready to go to the next level?
Are you ready to become successful?
Are you truly ready to get out of your own way?

Nothing would give me more pleasure than to help you succeed and go to the next level in your personal and/or business life.

To learn more about Coaching, Energy Healing, Speaking and Various Resources provided by Patricia LeBlanc

Then visit www.LoaLifeCoaching.com
Of www.TalkwithPatricia.com

THE END